JILL JOHNSTON

THE DISINTEGRATION OF A CRITIC

Edited by
Fiona McGovern, Megan Francis Sullivan, Axel Wieder

Bergen Kunsthall

Published by Bergen Kunsthall and Sternberg Press
on the occasion of the exhibition

Jill Johnston. The Disintegration of a Critic
Bergen Kunsthall
23 May – 11 August 2019
Curated by Fiona McGovern, Megan Francis Sullivan, Axel Wieder

Reprints of the texts by Jill Johnston with kind permission of
the Jill Johnston Literary Archive.

Texts: Bruce Hainley, Jennifer Krasinski, Ingrid Nyeboe
Editors: Fiona McGovern, Megan Francis Sullivan, Axel Wieder
Transcription and Copy Editing: Kerstin Rode, Elise Hunchuck
Design: HIT
Printing: Nørhaven, Dänemark

ISBN 978-3-956794-89-6

Distributed by The MIT Press, Art Data, and Les presses du réel

Sternberg Press
Caroline Schneider
Karl-Marx-Allee 78
10243 Berlin, Germany
www.sternberg-press.com

Bergen Kunsthall
Rasmus Meyers allé 5
5015 Bergen, Norway
www.kunsthall.no

Published in collaboration with Artists Space, New York
www.artistsspace.org

SternbergPress

BERGEN KUNSTHALL

CONTENTS

FOREWORD

This publication is dedicated to the writing of the cultural critic, auto/biographer and lesbian icon Jill Johnston (1929–2010). Starting in the early 1960s, Johnston made a name for herself as the author of a popular dance column in the New York-based weekly newspaper *The Village Voice*. It soon became one of the most important chronicles for the Judson Dance Theater and other happenings in the city's downtown scene. From the late 1960s onwards, her column oozed out of an objective critical standpoint and set the stage for the emergence of Johnston as a public figure and self-proclaimed radical lesbian that defied any prescribed position. Over more than fifteen years, the column interwove forms and formats, political, literary, art-historical and critical positions, taking turns and loops, reflecting its times and contexts.
As a person and writer, Johnston pioneered a model that not only challenged established notions of professional roles, but performed and created a new lesbian identity: "Everybody wanted to 'be' Jill Johnston," Eileen Myles remembered in a recent conversation. It was the platform of writing that enabled this body of work, and a collapse of distinction between personal, critical, and political, to unfold and create such a lasting effect.

Despite its broad influence at the time, and on later generations of writers and critics, Johnston's writing has not been in print for some time. The core of this publication includes thirty texts by Jill Johnston, selected from over 200 columns published in *The Village Voice* between 1960 and 1974, some of which were reprinted in collections during her lifetime, such as *Marmalade Me* (1971), *Gullibles Travels* (1974) and the radical-feminist classic *Lesbian Nation* (1973). Johnston's column started under the title "Dance," and followed the modern dance practices of Merce Cunningham, Aileen Passloff and Martha Graham before it picked up on the activities at Judson Church, with Freddie Herko, Yvonne Rainer and many others. Shifting to "Dance Journal" in 1965, Johnston's focus broadened to include happenings, Fluxus events and other art activities. Observations around the context of dance events or art activities, their impact on her (which sometimes included her own participation), or the economic or social conditions of the scene, feature as prevalently in her texts as the works themselves.

From the early 1970s onwards, her column was simply called "Jill Johnston," and there was no longer an attempt to confine her observations to any one determined category. At this point, the columns became significantly longer, using only lower-case spelling and/or no punctuation. They shifted in tone from political polemic, stream-of-consciousness, letter form, and personal anecdote—sometimes all mixed into one. Critical observations around motherhood, the women's movement, lesbian identity, media representations, and politics became central in her writing. The selection of Jill Johnston's texts in this publication reflects the moves and narratives of her writing, specifically as it unfolded in her long-term and regular column—a format that enabled the author and her readers a field of adventure, transformation, and exchange. While Johnston was and is often known either as a dance critic or the author of *Lesbian Nation*, we hope to bring the multifarious aspects of her work together, by focusing on her writing as a platform where the boundaries between performance, criticism, and life are realigned.

This selection of Jill Johnston's columns is accompanied by three texts written for this publication that speak about the author and her relevance. Her long-time partner and spouse Ingrid Nyeboe contributes personal memories of Johnston's style and impact as a writer, while writer Bruce Hainley reflects on the present vitality of her language. Writer, critic, and editor Jennifer Krasinski considers Johnston's work through a wider biographical framework, including her work for other magazines and publications.

An appendix collects historical material connected to a single event that also supplies the title of this book: a panel discussion that Johnston organized in 1969—precisely fifty years ago—at Loeb Center of New York University titled "The Disintegration of a Critic: An Analysis of Jill Johnston." Participants included Andy Warhol, Ultra Violet, Charlotte Moorman, Carolee Schneemann, Gregory Battcock and others, moderated by David Bourdon, while Johnston herself made a surprise appearance. While the event was enacted as a public departure for Johnston from her role as a critic, putting her own persona center stage, it can also be seen as a complex performative reflection on the changing role of criticism, or discourse, in art.

We are thankful for the help that we received at all stages of this project, and it was touching to meet many people to whom Jill Johnston meant a lot, personally and professionally. We are grateful for the contributions to this publication, and the work of the designers HIT, Lina Grumm and Annette Lux. We want to mention that an initial introduction to the writing of Jill Johnston came through the artists Ken Okiishi and Nick Mauss. Our most special thanks are for Ingrid Nyeboe, who trusted us in producing this book.

Fiona McGovern, Megan Francis Sullivan, Axel Wieder

Part 1

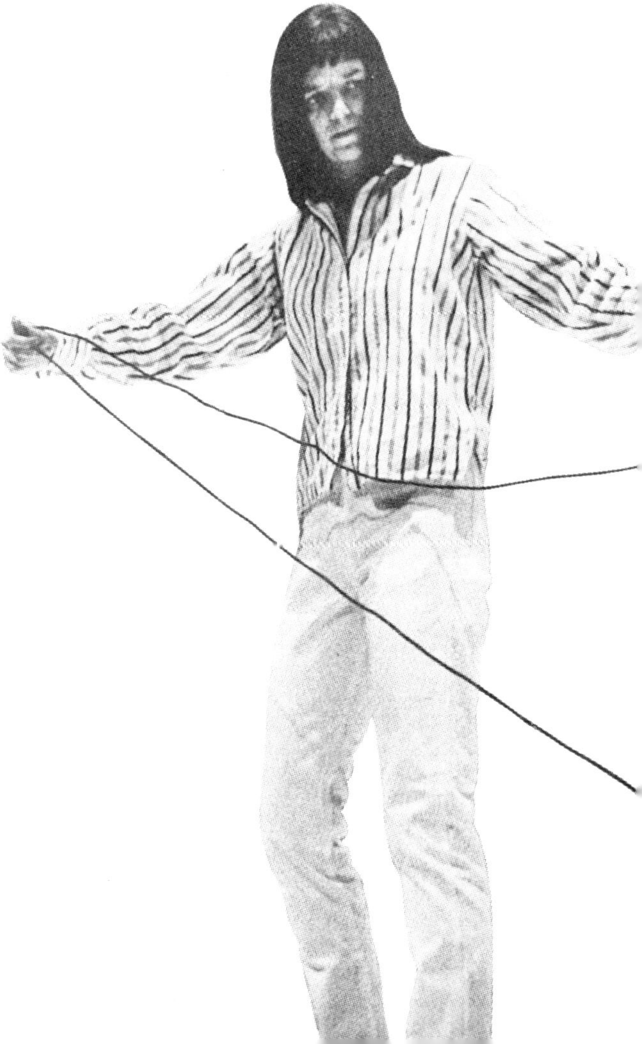

A selection of columns from The Village Voice: 1960–1974

Grammar and spelling of the texts by Jill Johnston follow the formatting of the initial publication in *The Village Voice*. Only minor editorial adjustments were made.

AILEEN PASSLOFF & CO.

1960-03-02

Aileen Passloff presented an intriguing collection of dances at the Living Theater the evening of February 22. Glancing over the titles after the concert, I enjoyed myself thinking of those strange bedfellows on the same program together, and imagining them all mixed together in one opus. To imagine such a mixture is not a daring feat because Miss Passloff's point of departure *is* the dissolution of conventional connections. Be that as it may, the subject matter of her dances as stated in the titles is consistently adhered to. The movements appear in piecemeal fashion; nothing is continuous, there are no phrases, something happens here, period—then there, period, and so on. But the pieces offered different aspects, or qualities, of the subject. This is true of "Battle Pieces," "At Home," and "A Dance of Sleep." Also of James Waring's dance on the program, a solo for Miss Passloff called "A Swarm of Butterflies Encountered on the Ocean," a soft lovely dance with curves, smiles, and flutters.

"At Home" was Miss Passloff's most extended dance having to do with a subject. It is really quite an intense drama, a psychological drama. Very absorbing. The Home atmosphere is set with a lurid green light dangling from the flies, and an ironing board and a chair placed beneath it. Nobody is very happy in this dance. The "family" is spent, weary, down-at-the-mouth, hateful and suspicious. One of the girls, with lots of hair and a dazed expression, seems to be out of her mind (an exceptional performance by Joan Baker). Miss Passloff moves her dance forward with a number of "poses" and a series of "incidents" in which the dancers suggest a variety of taunting and cynical relationships between each other, or simply establish themselves somehow in isolation from the others, perhaps with ridiculous or obscene gestures. The dance culminates in a "musical celebration." From a bag Miss Passloff desultorily hands out a few sad-sounding, beepy instruments, and that's all—they beep a little in an aimless circle.

The new dance for group, "Cypher," is heavy and black, also massive and static. The small stage of the Living Theater is not an adequate place to show it, unless Miss Passloff intends the increased suffocation which results from all that density packed in a small space. But I think it needs more room to convey the visual interest which seems important to the dance, and it is a fine enough piece to deserve a better frame.

CUNNINGHAM IN CONNECTICUT

1961-09-07

The annual Dance Festival at New London this year (August 17–20) employed eight choreographers, four older, four younger, and the warring camps remain as decisive as ever in their convictions as to who is really it and who isn't, but that's what camps do. For myself, Merce Cunningham, his dances and dancers, are greater than ever—like aging wine they taste better every year—and I consider myself fortunate to be a spectator in this era of a dancer-choreographer with the genius, integrity, breadth (all those words) to keep alive, in touch and to be making always experiences which ask no more of the observer than a desire to see.

NOT EASY TO SEE

It is not easy to see. Outside the theatre, living as we do, most of us see very little with our eyes wide open. In action the eye absorbs space forms to function; in repose the eye becomes a facial decoration as sight turns inward. And our training is such that when we do look for non-functional reasons, it is usually at something huge and spectacular, like cathedrals or sunsets. And even then it is rare to see more than a general outline. Or to see more and still *enter*. That is the crucial transition, from seeing to entering. Not only crucial but mysterious, so I won't say any more except to note that I think most people who go to dance concerts don't see very well, not even dancers, sometimes dancers especially, and most often critics, who must attend special classes in becoming blind.

Mr. Cunningham presented a new dance "Aeon," almost 50 minutes long, to a score by John Cage and with décor by Robert Rauschenburg. "Aeon" is a dance of great scale. It moves through so much, in range of quality, physical force, the human condition, that the whole thing is staggering to think of in retrospect. Human events: the activity of dancers on a proscenium stage. Other human events: the ways people communicate with each other, or speak for themselves. Exterior events: explosions, clouds, lights, a machine, sounds. And always the dancing, the superb dancing. The stillness too, which is never a mere choreographic stop, but an act of undaunted containment, of simple yet magnificent composure, of not being which is the essence of being. A complete act, not a choreographic or dramatic transition. Yet Cunningham the choreographer is a man who certainly knows what to do next. It is downright satisfying to participate in a sweep of tremendous agitation, like the sequence near the beginning of "Aeon" of high jumps and falls—the whole company moving off stage right as they jump and fall, the arms and head also involved in side-to-side movements, the bodies heaving up and down in counter rhythms—which leaves just Cunningham on the stage standing, looking at one fallen girl in a silent aftermath.

Cunningham's own range in this dance is fantastic. Not only those typical sudden shifts from motion to stillness, but the subtle gradations of energy, (I have a vivid recollection of an "incident" originating as a vibration in the thighs, transferred to the stomach, traveling upwards into the arms and shoulders and exploding like a geyser at the top); not to mention all the complicated coordinations, and the wordless drama that every movement event secretes.

Cunningham is a great dancer, and you know it not by his technical range and command alone; you feel it in the whole man, the whole man is in it every time. You may see a procession of selves and the man never makes a move not true to himself.

The Cunningham style of composition has exerted its influence, with some interesting results, but none so interesting as a dance on the Festival by Ruth Currier titled "Resonances." Miss Currier evidently decided to solve her "problem" (a tragedy involving four people—it is impossible to follow these plots without explicit program notes) with two solutions: the first in the grief-stricken velvet-and-gown style; the second, I take it, in a Currier version of Cunningham—leotard, tights, Non-Objective. This curious imitation revealed a long miscalculating attitude of many artists towards Cunningham's work, that his dances are de-humanized, de-personalized, abstract, non-objective if you will. Take the red blood of a living style and inject it with pure doses of Idea. Result: poison, disease, a de-humanized abstraction. What a buckling irony!

Anna Sokolow's kind of expressionism is direct, immediate, and, in a dance like "Dreams," hypnotic. Miss Sokolow doesn't pull any punches. The tension is right there, bam, raw, undistilled. I think you feel it that way for two reasons.

Once she draws out a movement image she pulls every bit of juice out of it—through hypnotic repetitions and intense performance. Second, the image itself is usually a primordial product; it has a kinesthetic power corresponding to deep springs of tension—the self-preservative emotions of attraction and repulsion. (I am reminded of T. S. Eliot's Objective Correlative for poetry.) Miss Sokolow makes a high concentrate of one image, dwells on it, makes it go, sometimes propels it into an orgasmic release. The hypnotic effect breaks down only when the choreographer is too impressed with an image to let it go.

DEMOCRACY

1962-08-23

It was a democratic evening of dance at Judson Memorial Church on July 6. There were 14 choreographers and 17 performers. There should have been something for everybody, including a nap if desired; and in fact there was so much that special moments arose as expected and at least three dances provoked a big response from everybody.

I liked Fred Herko's "Once or Twice a Week I Put on Sneakers to Go Uptown." Herko did a barefoot Suzie-Q in a tassel-veil head-dress, moving around the big open performing area (no stage at the church) in a semi-circle, doing only the barefoot Suzie-Q with sometimes lazy arm snaking up and collapsing down.

BUSINESS AT HAND

John Herbert McDowell is a composer. He has no dance training. He made a dance called "February Fun at Bucharest." Having no tics or tensions arising from a training and having an inordinate sense of fun, McDowell distinguishes himself as a "natural"—not a natural dancer (although you could think of it that way if you're not too set in your idea of what dancing is); I mean a natural person going about the business at hand, which in this case consisted of a few zany actions performed in a red sock and a yellow sweater.

Ruth Emerson is a tall, imposing woman who makes simple, direct, clean movement and occasionally ruins it with a gesture that doesn't look like hers. If the gesture turns up by chance it must be a problem to internalize it. Chance procedures (which predominated in this program) are useful in many ways and usually produce novel results, but in the end the only thing that matters is who is doing what. Chance procedures are preliminary controls: the chance results are subjected to the control of performance, and that means you always end up with a person expressing himself. Movement is not like sound in that respect. Movement is the person. The material and the person are One.

David Gordon, for instance. For my free time David Gordon did two extraordinary dances on that program. He did some movement nobody ever saw before. Like the body bent off center, the head awkwardly strained back, the elbows squeezed into the ribs as the flattened hands and forearms made the painful beauty of spastic helplessness. As though the body were straining, yelling, against an involuntary violence. Molloy and Malone should be so lucky.

AFTER THE DROUGHT

William Davis came up with dance No. 13, "Crayon," to some jazz: Dee Clark, the Shells, and the audience went crazy for a minute because of the dry spell that came before. I think the audience was glad enough to see Davis, too. He's a finely proportioned dancer who performs with quiet, clean, unassuming strength. And the dance was a good one. I only wish he had let loose, just once anyway.

Not that it mattered so much. And then Yvonne Rainer came on with "Ordinary Dance." It was an ordinary dance because it is autobiographical and Miss Rainer does a lot of talking while she moves, ordinary-type talking, telling you the facts (Hugo St. … oh yes I forgot to mention Gilroy the two wheel cart that moved the earth … 1941–1942 … let's see … uh … panhandle, early morning, white … I'm really not telling you much am I …). Poetry of facts. The title has its ironic aspect. The dance is out of the ordinary. Like Gordon she did some movement nobody ever saw before. I can't say any more now except the audience responded tumultuously and we had good reason.

Also on the program, and not discussed for reasons of space, were dances by Steve Paxton, Elaine Summers, Carol Scothorn, Gretchen MacLane, and Deborah Hay. I didn't mention that this was an important program in bringing together a number of young talents who stand apart from the past and who could make the present of modern dance more exciting than it's been for twenty years (except for an individual here and there who always makes it regardless of the general inertia). Almost all these dancers and choreographers were in Robert Dunn's composition class at the Living Theatre.

JUDSON CONCERTS #3, #4

1963-02-28

Concert Dancers No. 3 and No. 4 appeared at Judson Memorial Church on January 29 and 30. The revolution in dance is upon us. The revolution has been going on for fifteen years. But now the numbers of people are impressive. Just a little over a year ago you could still despair over the rare occasions when you might see the few isolated choreographers who made anything worthwhile because they were proceeding (and continue) alone to make dance within themselves and of the present moment. In the Judson concerts there is a big, pliable, inchoate matrix of independent, original activity which knows itself even while looking for itself: The core of dancer-choreographers engaging in these concerts, as well as those who drop in and out, constitute a kind of loose, free-wheeling phalanx which is more than enough to fill that uncomfortable vacuum left by the decline, around 1945, of the first modern dance.

INDISCRIMINATION

One of the good things about the Judson concerts is the indiscriminate attitude of including just about as many dancers or non-dancers (in as many kinds of actions and movement) as seem willing to participate. The programs may tighten up later on, but for the moment a certain amount of indiscrimination makes the most encouraging situation for everybody concerned. If that sounds provisional, I would add that I think it's great to be as inclusive as possible, because it's more like life that way. On a large, unwieldy program many experiences are available, and you can love it or hate it or fall asleep and not be too concerned about getting your trouble's worth every foot of the time.

Be that as it may, there have been enough dancers on these programs to make the boat rock with dangerous excitement. The possibilities of form and movement have become unlimited. There is no one way to make a dance; there is no kind of movement that can't be included in these dances; there is no kind of sound that is not proper for accompaniment. Only the integrity of the performer is at stake, the integrity to do the business at hand, to be inside that business, so that the action and the performer become one. The sluggish run of a non-dancer can be as moving and important as the beautifully extended leap of a dancer.

RUNNING DANCE

Yvonne Rainer opened the first program with a running dance ("We Shall Run," to the Berlioz "Requiem") performed by twelve dancers and non-dancers. Standing in a line, before they began to run, with impassive attention, they looked like what they were: people. No "attitudes," just waiting to execute the plan. Then they ran, an even jog (not always in step, of course), running and running, back and forth across the gymnasium, moving in compact groups—a pervasive collective feeling, as the rhythm accumulated insistence, that finally bloomed absolutely heroic. The heroism of the ordinary. No plots or pretensions. People running. Hurray for people.

Miss Rainer also repeated "Three Seascapes." And she danced in many other pieces, including Steve Paxton's "Words Words." Aside from her extraordinary "presence" and technical command, Miss Rainer is the most independent choreographer of this particular scene. To be more general about it, I think she's the greatest thing since Isadora crossed the Atlantic, or St. Denis saw that Egyptian cigarette poster, or any other important moments you can think of in the lives of several astonishing ladies a few decades ago.

Mr. Paxton and Miss Rainer danced the former's "Words Words" naked—that is, naked except for one or two items required by law. The exposure was a natural extension (removal) of the revealing tights and leotards most dancers wear. And if the shock at first distracted from the dance, the novelty wore of soon enough and you were left with two bodies (you could watch the bodies, too) in a dance that was classically pure and not terribly interesting. Mr. Paxton rested against the wall while Miss Rainer performed a solo of about thirteen phrases. She rested and he performed the same solo. Then they both did it together. If the length of the dance and the absence of contact (neuter, sexually) were meant to offset the nudity, I didn't mind. But I wouldn't have minded some relationship either. Since they both performed with total clarity and self-possession, anything would seem possible, in retrospect at least.

Mr. Paxton also danced with Judith Dunn in her duet "Index," to music of intermittent mouth sounds composed by Robert Dunn. This is a long, impressive dance combining many rigorous or lyric phrases and "events." What I liked especially was a phrase near the beginning when Miss Dunn leans against her partner, looks at him long and soft, turns and slides slowly down his torso. Aside from the beauty of contact, I liked it because it was one of the few moments when Miss Dunn relaxed from the neck up. As a dancer of fine command and technical accomplishment, she could afford to be more indulgent. Another arresting episode was jagged succession of tense pretended balances followed by lunges of one at the other around the neck to make both collapse and crash on the floor.

BEING READY

This sequence reminds me a little of Trisha Brown's duet "Lightfall," also performed with Steve Paxton. Using the simple action of waiting (football style, hands on knees) as a recurrent "base," the dancers initiated a spontaneous series of interferences—ass-bumping and back-hopping—which were artless, playful excursions in quiet expectancy and unusual surprises. Miss Brown has a genius for improvisation, for being ready when the moment calls, for being "there" when the moment arrives. Such facility is no mere tongue-wagging, but the result of an interior calm and confidence and of highly developed kinesthetic responses. She's really relaxed and beautiful.

Another long duet was William Davis's "Field," performed with Barbara Lloyds, accompanied by transistor radios (stations WABC and WINS) attached to their waists. Like Miss Dunn's dance it was rigorous, demanding, and well done, though more derivative in its movement. I have to mention that just when they came lyrically together Miss Lloyd's radio decided to broadcast "Moon River."

SPICED LILACS

Elaine Summers' "Suite" is funny and well-timed, much better than the Woodstock version. Ruth Emmerson's "Giraffe" is expansive, extended, easy, controlled. Lucinda Child's "Pastime" is an intense, cryptic solo of three episodes, including a very difficult part, moving so slowly, seated in a piece of manipulated material. Deborah Hay's "City

Dance," for group, is an imaginative abstraction of hurried motion in complex, dispersed patterns. Carol Scothorn's "The Lazarite" communicated the idea that "there is no death."

Fred Herko's "Little Gym Dance Before the Wall for Dorothy" is a wonderful vignette: coming in straight out down the middle, removing jacket and boots, and sauntering off casually straight out down the middle. And Arlene Rothlein—she was a sweet breath of spiced lilacs in her solo "It Seemed to Me There Was Dust in the Garden and Grass in My Room." I loved this mixed-up patchwork piece, even though several transitions were awkward because a few gestures were not truly assimilated.

Additional attractions on both programs were: Carolee Schneeman's mad orgy "Newspaper-Event"; Bob Huot and Bob Morris dressed (smothered) in the most incredible, gorgeous panoply and trying to kill each other for real in "War" (La Monte Young beating a steady, resounding gong); and an amazing musical event, "Certain Distilling Processes," by Philip Corner, employing four dancers as conductors and seventeen intriguing persons making noise with instruments of many descriptions.

YVONNE RAINER: I

1963-05-23

On April 28 and 29 Yvonne Rainer presented a new work for six dancers at Judson Memorial Church. "Terrain," a long dance in five sections, is a brilliant culmination of a style and method that Miss Rainer has been exploring in short pieces over the past year or so. After the concert on the 29th a friend of the choreographer exuberantly congratulated me for having said a while back that Miss Rainer will be the next Martha

Graham. I didn't, in fact, say that at all, so after I reminded the friend of what I actually wrote, he went on to say that at the time he thought it was unfair to place a "burden" on a young artist with grand prophecies (my words), but that he now agreed with me and thought Miss Rainer was equal to any ... what, challenge, I think he said.

THE NEXT RAINER

Actually, in that review of the last Judson Church concerts I made a statement and not a prophecy. If I had to say Miss Rainer would be the next anything, I'd say she would be the next Yvonne Rainer. However, by indulging in a historical reference, I realize that I was dabbling in a notorious occupational absurdity of critics. In the case of Miss Rainer, now that I think of it, the absurdity is based on a simple rationale. As spokesman I believe I was expressing the enthusiasm of a number of people who, like myself, have been pleasurably involved in the progress and doings of a certain group of dancers and who recognized in Miss Rainer, participating in that group from the beginning, an unusual personality of fertile imagination, with the drive and intelligence to project in objective terms an individual style, derived from the immediate past, with original modifications and advances.

In "Terrain" Miss Rainer sustained all her interests in a work of great dimension. Each of the five sections of the dance could be performed as self-sufficient dances (except the last section, perhaps, which is a kind of coda). Thus the total event is like stringing beads, or putting panels together, the way some painters do. Integration is a matter of stylistic consistency. Pacing may be important in sustaining interest. For Miss Rainer the pacing results from a combination of her own set phrases, which have great qualitative variety, and the indeterminate continuity of those phrases arising from a method which permits the dancers to choose the sequence of those phrases and the space in which he will perform them. However, since "Dance for Three People and Six Arms" of last year, Miss Rainer has elaborated this method to include signals and ground rules, thereby adding the freedom of "calling the play," so to speak, and imposing the restriction of obeying the signal according to the rules of the game. For example, "Diagonal," the opening section for group, consists of fourteen set activities (all travelling on the two diagonals), each one designated by a letter or a number. The performer may choose any activity he likes and perform it on the diagonal when he happens to be in a corner, or he may call a number or a letter and if anybody else happens to be at that corner at the same time they must perform the activity designated by that signal with the dancer who called it. Complexity arises from further rules specifying how the performer may join the diagonal activity when he is "walking" or "standing still" in the general space (any performer may walk or stand still when he is not dancing on the diagonal).

MORE RULES

The fourth section, called "Play," is more elaborate in rules and signals (words in this case) and the complexity of the actual phrases. The ground base of the section is the "ball phrase," a different one being assigned to each performer, who may do his or somebody else's or call somebody else and tell them what to do. He may also call for a red ball from a supplier in the balcony whenever he feels like it, if not engaged in a specific activity. Needless to say, each performance of these group sections will differ in many details—of continuity, pacing, quality, and spatial relationships.

It is interesting to note how Miss Rainer has here developed an original scheme based on the complex, refined chance methodology of Merce Cunningham (who is as responsible as anybody for the recent breakthrough of exciting dance business). Cunningham's procedure, which he has not used exclusively, is to set all the components of the dance—the movements and their situation in space and time—by the use of charts representing a large number of possibilities of those components, and tossing coins to determine, at each step, which possibility should occur. Miss Rainer, on the other hand, makes certain choices to begin with and transposes the chance operation into the actual performance of the dance. Chance here becomes improvisatory. The total method is a combination of set material with directives for the free, spontaneous use of that material, limited by rules which further enhance or restrict the freedom of the performer.

INHERENT REPETITION

The constant repetition of material is inherent in this method. Of the two sections mentioned above I enjoyed "Play" more because, at second seeing anyway, the greater complexity of rules and material pushed both the method and the repetitions further from mind. Miss Rainer does not intend to hide the method, which is as integral to the performance as the signals of a catcher to his pitcher are integral to a baseball game, but I have more fun when I'm confused. I rarely made an actual connection between a signal and its referent, but in "Diagonal" I became too familiar with the "plan" like a bell for breakfast. In "Play" a lot of action came into vision from noplace, so to speak; thus the material was more fragmented. I don't mind seeing the same material many times. Life keeps going on and no time is the same. But when a style of movement is so individual and assertive, as Miss Rainer's is, I get a little weak when I see it so clearly so often, and then I feel like retreating, or having it retreat from me, which happens in "Play" because the whole thing is more mixed up.

THE OBJECT

1964-05-21

Writing a short piece recently about a new dance scene, with the emphasis on works made by artists, I was suddenly confounded by the absence of a lever to describe just how the artists have been involved in dance. Then somebody mentioned the magic word "objects." So I arbitrarily decided that the point at which artists have become performers and choreographers is the moment of transition from a static construction to the kind of construction that invites manipulation. That seems clear enough, and I had momentarily forgotten that the Happenings by the painters were mobilized Environments. The performers in the Happenings were almost always manipulation objects.

INVITATION TO ATTACK

In an exhibition at Cordier and Ekstrom this winter, Jim Dine had a nostalgic reminder of his Happenings in the form of a canvas with a hatchet on a chain stuck in a rough beam of wood which divided the canvas down the middle. The implicit invitation to attack the wood was not lost on many, I heard that the work was destroyed in no time.

Dine's hatchet canvas was one of many object-constructions shown around the galleries these past few years which invite participation by the observer. The participation changes the character of the work or leaves it essentially intact. In either case the construction and the participant became collaborators in an Event. The next step is the relative formality of presenting the Event before a captive audience. No doubt the next step after that should be an invitation to the audience to close in on this transplanted audacity, an outcome toward which we might do well to strive. Actually, this has been done, but on a selective basis, which makes sense in terms of numbers if total annihilation does not seem desirable.

SINGULAR FACTS

Two recent works presented on a series by the Judson Dance Theatre, April 27-29, reveal the extent to which the artists and dancers of the Judson group have been grappling with objects these past two or three years. Lucinda Childs' "Carnation" and Robert Morris "Site" are impeccable object-events with a short but eminent history behind them. Objects have figures in many works in all manner of loose and restrictive handling. They have been presented and manipulated as simple, singular facts, and they have been exploited as to their associative potential. "Site" and "Carnation" are works of maximum efficiency with a high-tension charge in their power to evoke feeling behind a neutral facade. At least two previous works by Judson Dunn's "Acapulco"; the other was an earlier piece by Morris, "Arizona."

With "Site" Morris extends himself juxtaposing three elements. Dressed in white, wearing work gloves and a skin-tight, flesh-colored mask, Morris stands before a white box containing a tape recorder which makes the constant rumbling sound of a pneumatic drill (previously recorded from his studio window). To his right is a stack of three large rectangular plywood boards, painted white. He removes one and stands it up vertically a few yards away. He removes the second and takes it off-stage. After a few moments he returns, grasps a corner of the third, and pulls it away swiftly to reveal a reclining odalisque, backed with white pillows, her skin covered in faint white make-up so that she looks somewhat dewy and transparent. She is also a facsimile of Manet's "Olympia." Morris makes the famous Manet painting his "found" object as a live entity on the stage. She remains transfixed while he manipulates the plywood board, making a moving sculpture of body and object, with the additional visual effect of shifting relationships between Morris, the odalisque, the small white box, and the stationary vertical board. Morris is a workman performing tasks of balance and control. The pneumatic drill corroborates his activity. Both are dramatically opposed to the ideal poetic image of the transfixed lady. After the initial shock of exposure, the slow revelation of association sets in. Nobody is immune to the cultural significance. The extreme neutrality—the visual emphasis, the matter-of-fact manipulation, the absence of contact—is the work of an artist putting different pictures, like photographs, together on a canvas and letting the audience take it from there.

Lucinda Childs worked her materials in "Carnation" with a similar economy and precision, but unlike Morris she pushed the facts into a fanciful absurdity of slight horror and some pathos. She sits at a small table with a visage of contained intensity, contemplating a plan of action with foam-rubber curlers and sponges, as momentous as a call to battle. She puts the curlers between the sponges, places a salad colander on her head, pulls out each curler with a neat swift pull, and places them around her head on the prongs of the colander. That done, she sticks the sponges in her mouth, removes the curlers, the colander, gets up and dumps them with unceremonious relief into a blue plastic bag, into which she injects her foot. The next section involves a head stand, a sheet, and two socks (attached to the sheet) with some difficult maneuvering. Finally, she caps this perfect and meticulous nonsense with a meaningless assault on the blue plastic bag. After careful placement of the bag she runs towards it, jumps on it, stands immobilized, glares in frenetic silence until her face starts to cry, and at the final moment of wrinkled distortion returns to deadpan normal and prepares for another attack on the bag.

FLUXUS FUXUS

1964-07-02

Fluxus flapdoodle. Fluxus concert, 1964. Donald Duck meets the Flying Tigers. Why should anyone notice the shape of a watch at the moment of looking at the time? Should we formulate the law of the fall of a body toward a center, or the law of the ascension of a vacuum toward a periphery? The exposition became a double Bloody Mary. Some Fluxus experts went to the Carnegie Tavern also. Fluxus moved into the street and on to my typewriter. Polyethelene and people everywhere and some of them have all these voices, Soren Agenoux said (that). The voice of being kind to your fine feathered friends. Put your favorite sounds in a tube and see how they come out at the other end. Be kind to Your Fine Feathered Friends was never so palatable. Take a loaf of Tip-Top bread and try constructing a staircase. What did George Macunias mean by saying that "all other pieces have been performed whether you notice them or not"? I noticed George Macunias enter formally (what is the name of the high round collar you see the men wearing in those old photos, sitting stiffly for posterity) with a French horn but I couldn't determine from the balcony what fell out of the horn when he bowed. Stones or marbles. They rolled. The sound of stones or marbles rolling. lt might also be amusing to see the King in his finery walk down the aisle formed by his silent obedient courtiers, turn to prepare to be seated on the throne, and retch. For that to which we are accustomed, prepare to die. What could anybody expect from a French horn in a Fluxus concert at the Carnegie Recital horn, uh, hall. Horns and halls. And the orchestra seated as well known, leader, conductor, immaculate in tails, Kuniharu Akiyama, famed possibly for his interpretations of contemporary music. Silence, order in the court. Arms uplifted. The signal. The single sound. Curtain. The sound of one sound sounding. Another an historic occasion. No, it is not like the baby crying I hear now outside my window. It is exactly like a sound made in the Carnegie Recital Hall made at approximately 10 P.M. Historical as a pumpkin pie. What do my expectations have to do with rolling marbles?

Consider Nam June Paik, Korean expatriot, active in Europe. I knew about his violin piece. I knew he stood behind a table holding a violin in two hands and raised it so slowly overhead and at the zenith brought it down to crash and be destroyed by impact with table. That was the form I expected. But Paik might have surprised himself as well as me. The audience was already giddy from making their own music (laughter) apart from what they might have thought to be the absence of it where they had any reason to expect it from a historical setting of elegant high purpose. Already they had witnessed the wind music of five musicians watching the air from the wings blow gently some sheets of paper off their music stands. And George Brecht placing a vase of flowers (later at the Carnegie Tavern) on the grand piano. And Alison Knowles explaining her Child Art Piece which had been done in Paris and Düsseldorf but which was canceled here to conform to the tenets of the Society for the Prevention of Cruelty to Children and replaced by Version 2: Exit in a New Suit. And Philip Corner at the piano submitting the image of himself, precise placements of hands, no sounds. And a piece for three, four-stringed instruments by Congo, chimpanzee from London. So that if Paik did not want to surprise himself he might have done his work of taut concentration at the outset. A stringed instrument can cost a fortune. Everybody knows that. How much can it cost to change your mind? Paik changed his mind when his arms and violin were extended parallel to the floor. At the moment he stepped aside, spoke briefly, possibly in a white fury, and if so smashed the violin out of a present need, more present than the fulfillment of a planned action. Pure Fluxus. Did LaMonte Young know he was going to burn a violin in a concert at Ninety-first Street several years ago? Modes of destruction and positive statement. What about the excellent fad of college boys which began in Derby, England, and moved on to California where the boys organized a Piano Reduction Study Group to reduce the piano in the shortest possible time to such a state that it may be passed through an aperture of twenty cm. in diameter? The record time was 10 minutes 44.4 seconds. What is to be said about this or about the gradual erosion of a piano left to nature's design in a junkyard? One could observe and record the phenomenon in either case. Is Child Art on the stage any different from Child Art in the home? Of course it is, and Fluxus fux any notion of value attached to staying home or going to the theatre. Fluxus composers are contemporary Pataphysicians. Pataphysics is the science of particulars, the examination of laws which govern exceptions. The world is composed of exceptions, and it seems a shame to the Pataphysician to reduce the universe to unexceptional exceptions by discovering laws of the correlation of exceptions.

All things being exceptions it follows that each thing is a law unto itself, thus how could there be any competition for value among things which have no meaning beyond their own particular design? There can, therefore, only be indifference to value and not to the performance of a particular duty. Value resides in the performance. That is the elegant high purpose of it. No indifference, but engagement. Fluxus composers are not pro-art or anti-art. How could they be for or against anything when the thing to do on the program is to eat the hot dogs distributed by the conductor who caught them as they flew down to the stage on rope from the balcony? The action was also clear in Aye's Rainbow Piece for Wind Orchestra in which the conductor stabbed the bubbles made by instruments and a toy store bubble maker with his baton. Nor do I care about Fluxus one way or another. Going Fluxus was another engagement. It was a delightful occasion. Next time I might stay home, or contemplate a hot dog at Coney Island. Meanwhile, I salute you and fux Fluxus from the forty-two keys of my typewriter.

INSIDE "ORIGINALE"

1964-10-01

There was Allan Kaprow at one of those Avant-Garde Festival performances at Judson Hall coproduced by Charles Moorman and Norman Seaman and he was carrying a big sheaf of script or score which he said was the score for Stockhausen's "Originale," so somehow in a conversation during one number it was agreed that I might be an actor (one of five) since one of the actors was reluctant or out of town or indisposed. Next day Allan called me and said the actor was well or anxious or back in town and that therefore I might like to be a conductor. Next call I became an Actor again. But after Allan talked to Mary Baumeister, closely associated with the composer, he proposed as they agreed that I should be a free agent which later I discovered was what might have been called a "guest" since a personage called a "guest" was included in the score as an optional possibility by invitation of the director. As it developed there were several guests during the week of performances. Friday night the chimpanzee was ill and Mrs. X's daughter, who brought her two German Shepherds to the first performance, was out on Fifty-Seventh Street requesting the pleasure of an appearance of an elderly lady with her shaggy white dog to replace the chimp. The fourth night three unexpected guests made a rush on Nam June Paik, handcuffing him to a metal bar of the scaffolding. The three intruders were disposed of on the fire escape and locked out there. One of them was later found to be stuck head down in an apparatus on the roof. As a free agent I went to the last rehearsal just before the first performance to size up the situation. I looked at the score and asked a few questions about who was doing what when, etc. Stockhausen's score is that curious hybrid of control and indeterminacy common to works by many artists in the contemporary tradition of providing the possibility of unforeseen situations within a framework of instructions and temporal limitations. The framework for "Originale" consisted of strict time units for each action or performer. Thus an actor, according to specifications in the score, might have to appear at thirty minutes and depart at thirty-nine minutes (within the total time of ninety minutes). A further specification for an actor was that he choose selections from classical or modern drama to read or memorize for the performance. That left a wide margin of determination by the performer. Moreover, he could deliver his passages in whatever manner he desired. And I judged from the outfits, which changed night to night, that costume was similarly a matter of personal taste. Also, each actor had a bit of free time to do anything at all.

Along with the time structure, the sound score of the piece seemed absolutely determined. Stockhausen is best known in this country and abroad as an outstanding exponent of the new electronic music, produced on tape by a sinus generator. This technique was developed in the Studio for Electronic Music of the West German Radio under the direction of Herbert Eimert; and Stockhausen was one of five composers represented in the first performance of such compositions (1954). The electronic score for "Originale," notwithstanding the included score for live piano and percussion ensemble, was the single dominant and pervasive element of the work. Considering the hodgepodge of properties, animals, and assorted activities in the piece, the time structure was not a unifying factor but a method of insuring a change of pace throughout a lengthy composition.

My own idea when I went to the rehearsal was to assess the pace with a view to doing something when it seemed dynamically appropriate. As for what I would do exactly, I tried to be empty-headed about it in the spirit of improvisation, but I pondered the shape and footing of the scaffolding as one accessible instrument because I like to climb and hang on things. My only other thought was to interfere or make some relationship with the "painter" (time was allotted to a painter, who could do what he pleased), who made a big scene in a white outer-space gear standing on a ladder on the stage dropping raw eggs on the floor, shaking red pigment over the eggs, lying on a cot, laying a steamy stink bomb in a large can. I notified the painter of my intentions and he said to just be careful because he couldn't see very well through his cellophane visor; but if I had made some realistic account of the painter as the same fellow who walked around in regular clothes during the rehearsal flipping about the German Shepherds not being caged or leashed, I might have taken a quiet powder during his theatrical debut. The outcome, of course, after I had a good time crawling behind him into the recess under the stage, sitting on the floor pouring a little salt over his red pigment, adjusting a pair of white heels that happened to be there, and flailing the steam from the can with my hat, was that painter and wife, the following evening before the second performance, bore down on me with hot denouncements in the name of serious intentions and such jazz, which prompted Allan Kaprow to bear down on them in the name of grace and so on, while Allen Ginsberg, who had also been a subject of my happy interference the night before, sitting begoggled in gentle Buddhist indifference fingering some Eastern stringed instrument, remarked inaudibly that I could do whatever I liked with him, Jill. Well, what I decided about all this was that the psychology involved in indeterminacy is a complicated business. I recall somebody once asking John Cage, in a panel after a performance of new music, if he expected people to laugh at his piece, and Cage replied that he preferred laughter to tears. According to Mary Baumeister there was a fair amount of interplay or interference at the first performance of “Originale” in Cologne in 1961. Actually, I think more often than not in these compositions the performers are isolated in their respective activities. Indeterminacy in music has meant primarily the interpenetration of sound resulting from simultaneous juxtapositions of material from independent sources. In a typical indeterminate score by John Cage, each performer constructs his own program of action from the graphic notation accompanied by instructions. Such was his “Theatre Piece” (1960), an obvious precedent for “Originale.” As a piece of “theatrical music” the performers are expected “to be who they are (musician, dancer, singer, etc.) but the performer’s decision as to what he is to do will often be determined by whether he makes a sound.” Until recently, Cage’s indeterminacy consisted of an unforeseen situation made possible by the simultaneous presentation of actions and sounds produced by performers who brought their own scheme to the performance after determining that scheme by submitting their choices to certain chance operations. Lately Cage has relaxed these controls to push indeterminacy into the realm of improvisation (on-the-spot decisions) more familiar to dancers and jazz musicians. In 1962 I performed as the “dancer” with Cage and Tudor in the former’s “Music Walk.” I chose about forty-five actions mostly involving a load of household equipment, determining the sequence and time span for each action by the chance procedure indicated in the score. Armed with my forty-five cards I went to the rehearsal, but when I saw the lovely graphic designs on the cards of my colleagues and my own fell to the floor, dropped in the water, or some damn thing, I gave up on them and decided to move around from one coke bottle or frying pan to another during the performance. At that time such a course was not kosher in Cage's lexicon of behavior for the performer, who would do best to deliver himself from his own conventions (habitual preferences) by yielding to the external device of a chance procedure. However, it should be clear that habits are not so easily divested. One can force the issue by externally imposed strictures on time and sequence, but one is still left with that constant factor of the particular shape and volume of each body and the motion peculiar to that body. Cage looks like Cage to me no matter what he did beforehand to eliminate certain natural preferences in time and sequence. Moreover, the choice of equipment, determined by personal history, partially constitutes a "style," by which the composer is eventually identified. To be absurdly elementary about it, consider the fact that Cage goes on habitually making music. Life, in any case, is always a new mixture of habit and improvisation, and Cage is an inventor in a medium that he has made his habit. The "set" performances for a work like "Theatre Piece" make a set composition in a way as set as any traditional work. Cage's unique departure, of course, aside from the importance of extending music into a theatre of action, was to make the performer a composer in what amounts to a collective composition. Stockhausen's "Originale" is the same kind of work except that there is more freedom in certain respects and less in others. As mentioned above, the performer had no choice in the matter of time, a choice essential to Cage's position since Cage doesn't mind (philosophically) if the audience is bored, although he could conceivably depend on the law of averages to provide the pace that he refuses to set himself. In comparing "Theatre Piece" and "Originale," I am struck by one overwhelming difference in the two works. Cage's score is absolutely consistent in that its simple instructions apply to all performers alike and there is no extraneous material obtruded by the composer. Stockhausen's electronic score and other determined factors are hardly extraneous in the sense that they are commanding elements in the work; yet the obvious desire for "free" action is countered everywhere by controls and restraints which make even much of what is free look like a setup, which indeed it is, as in the case of Nam June Paik, whose performance was a solo specialty act and whose plunge into a tub of water, following a breathless silence during which the Korean composer stood in a spotlight saturating his face, neck, and collar with shaving cream and rice, was accompanied by a Wagnerian burst of electronic thunder. I agree with Earle Brown, who described Paik as a "kind of Oriental Kammerkrieg" (in a letter called "Planned Panichood"). Paik's specialty is much more than an act. But I'm talking about context and disposition in a collective work. I think Stockhausen's idea was to make a great theatrical "combine" of sound, movement, lights, colors, properties, and players, and he figured it out like a playscript with parts for friends and acquaintances, with sections providing a simultaneous overlap of activities, other sections providing a focus for a single activity, with the constant presence of plant and animal decor, electronic equipment, and technicians. Some people said it was a terrible mess. They also said, as the Times critic did, that there was much to admire. I know that it was an exciting occasion in Germany in 1961 as the first German happening. To some sophisticated New Yorkers, who have been through what Richard Bellamy refers to high-mindedly as the "classical" period of the happenings, "Originale" looked like a soup of ingredients from any number of familiar events. Sherman Drexler, for one, thinks that nobody should want to see another happening and that a sign at the exit should have read "This Way to the Egress," alluding to such a sign at the end of a Barnum and Bailey show of fake freaks. But "Originale" is not in the tradition of happenings as we know them by the painters (Dine, Oldenburg, Kaprow, Whitman, etc.). It is possible to make clean separations between one kind of event and another in a movement of international proportions deriving from one or two common sources (e.g., Cage); yet Stockhausen's work belongs essentially to the tradition of "theatrical music" realized on a more modest scale by certain American composers following Cage's suggestion. If "Originale" was a soup it was because Stockhausen mixed up three sizable components in his calculations. First, he wanted a Merz combine in which the Milky Way would have figured had it been feasible. Second, he is a composer, and his background as a composer is in a European deterministic tradition. The new electronic music offers a range of sound possibilities before unknown, but the composers in this medium have subjected their experiments to serial permutations traced back to the twelve-tone and serial techniques of Schönberg and Webern. Third, Stockhausen has been exposed to the attitudes and methods of Cagean indeterminacy and he wanted, as he has demonstrated in earlier compositions, some measure of free action by the performers. Thus the result was a weird triple exposure of chunks of set pieces (often having the mythopoeic quality of events in painterly happenings), a muddle of indeterminate confusion, and a pressure from clock and director to keep within the bounds of a meticulous score. I don't know why the Fluxus people were picketing the concert (somebody told me Fluxus committed suicide recently), but it might have been interesting if the director had invited the picket line to participate as "guests." From one guest to another (real or optional): I felt superfluous enough to guarantee that any intrusion could be welcome and horrible at the same time. Beyond that, as Duchamp once remarked and I have quoted before, perhaps the proceedings were "insufficiently light-hearted."

CRITICS' CRITICS

1965-09-16

Prompted by say something about the critic and his or her critic and critics and criticism in general and the modern necessity of reforming this ancient practice of pretending to be top man on a barber's pole. As I see it now, the land looks level enough to be a wide open field and I'm ready to run or walk on it without encountering a boogie man who wants to know if he looks tall enough and black enough to be a subject of one of my columns of lasting insignificance. In this respect I join two of my colleagues, John Wilcock and Jonas Mekas, and bow in passing, however reverentially, to Andrew Sarris who writes the best prose this side of James Agee. Criticism wears me out—it's like riding a bike up and down the country hills in a race against a phantom judge. I'll take a plot of level territory and stake out a claim to lie down on it and criticize the constellations if that's what I happen to be looking at. I also stake out a claim to be an artist, a writer, if that's what I'm doing when I get to the typewriter and decide that I liked something well enough to say what I think it's all about. I think one of the finest pieces of dance criticism or any criticism for that matter was a column written by Louis Horst the grand old man of "the moderne dance" two or three years before he died, in 1957 or '58 whenever it was that Paul Taylor presented that extraordinary concert, at the YM-YWHA, in which nothing very significant happened except that it was a concert by Paul Taylor and he stood still a lot or changed positions I'm not sure which it doesn't matter and I remember two girls in dresses and heels who stood still most of the time too and anyway Louis Horst presented his version of that concert—a blank column in the now defunct Dance Observer. I like that blank column because I think it meant that its originator was a bit stupefied by Paul Taylor's concert, prompting him (Horst) to present an honest version of a thing he couldn't see very well.

After all he was an old man and he'd weathered many early battles of the first modern dancers who also (like Taylor) had a rough time of it money-wise and all the other wises. Louis Horst's blank column might be taken as a model for the criticism of the future (by future I mean right now of course). One reason I'm writing this piece about criticism is that I just read Clive Barnes on criticism in the Times. With all respects to Mr. Barnes and I liked his article on criticism, I don't think of myself as a "parasite," which is the term Mr. Barnes used in referring to one who practices criticism. I was about to say:— one who practices the ART of criticism, which brings me back to what I said about staking out a claim to being an artist. And speaking of artists, why is it that more dancers don't practice the art of writing about their work? There's a long tradition of literacy among painters, composers, etc., and I see practically nothing on dance by dancers in public places. Walter Sorell once made a collection of essays by dancers ("The Dance Has Many Faces") and Merce Cunningham contributed an essay to an edition of "7 Arts" and of course Louis Horst always made it possible for dancers to contribute their writings to the Dance Observer and of course there are innumerable books in the Dance Collection of the New York Public Library, among them the autobiographies, but I mean more in the way of contemporary writings by contemporary dancer-choreographers. For instance, I also write for a magazine called Art News and over the years the "editorial associates" (reviewers, in effect) have been the artists as well as the writers who are not artists but who for some reason enjoy practicing the art of criticism. Need I say more? The field is wide open as I thought to mention in the beginning, thinking of how I feel about the difficulty of puffing your way up a steep hill on a bike that isn't motorized. The future is upon us and the Art of Criticism has already come into its own in those public places where the critic is lying down on a soft piece of ground to enjoy a bit of blue and yellow scenery … to be continued.

COMMUNICATIONS

1965-11-14

Last column I mentioned the issue of communications in dance. If there is just enough of whatever there is in the world it follows that systems of communication in dance are as sufficient as anything else. At the same time I see prospects of more making things merrier. I see a scope of action on many fronts, involving artists and spectators, beyond the present horizon. Adequate systems of communication are central to such expansion. Limited activities in dance correspond to the restricted means of communication by which new ideas are disseminated. Obviously, the financial economics of dance is pertinent. Dance is not property, not in the sense that painting and sculpture are materials of exchange in a supply and demand economy including all stabilized objects. Dances are not bought and sold. Dancers sell themselves as performers to ballet companies, musical comedy shows, and TV commercials. Modern dancers lease themselves to a choreographer for weeks of preparation (rehearsals) with no remuneration. If the choreographer is generous the dancer might receive $10 or $20 at the conclusion of the annual concert, which climaxes those weeks of grueling preparation. Choreographers can only hope to fill a theatre for the meagre box office returns that might cover the cost of production. If they're lucky and/or established they'll receive patronage in one form or another. George Balanchine has been patronized for many years, and although he is as established as any choreographer can hope to be, I doubt that his income even begins to approach the astronomical figures quoted in the market of painting. The low economy in the dance world is an index to the spare action in dance as compared to high level of participation and communication in other media. Especially in New York. Choreographers presenting work in New York can't make a penny. Merce Cunningham hasn't performed in

New York for several years. The last rumor of a Cunningham season in New York has depended upon a sum of $60,000 to rent a Broadway theatre for two weeks of repertory. The patrons are in the provinces. And if a choreographer wants to make a fair dime in the provinces he has to face the sacrifice of time and energy entailed in the discomforts of travelling and tedious organizational problems. Time for making new works is consumed by touring. Outside New York the choreographer also faces hostile audiences. Not always, but certainly not the readymade audiences of this advanced city. And the approving cliques in the city don't pay their choreographers until they've been around many years. At the recent Theatre Rally of young Judson choreographers a paying audience was solicited. They paid $3.50 per ticket or $15 for the series. Box office returns plus patronage covered the enormous costs of production, and the dancers received the privilege of performing, which I don't underestimate.

CIRCULAR

The problems are circular. A low economy is a cause of deficient communications and vice versa. In the provinces the choreographers are paid but the audiences are not informed. In the city the audiences tend to be informed but the choreographers are not paid. When the audiences are both rich and informed the choreographers will be in good shape. How is a public informed?—"In the rooms the women come and go, talking of Michaelangelo." In the galleries and museums, at the parties and in the bars, the people come and go, talking about the pictures, the price of the pictures, the reproduction of the pictures in national magazines, the latest editorials on the pictures, the latest fashions in lady artists, the latest fashions in collectors, the latest big openings, the new acquisitions, the future of a picture and all manner of facts pertaining to anybody's picture. In New York the picture scene is so big that the pictures are like the children in the shoe inhabited by the woman who had so many (children) she didn't know what to do. If the dance scene was a fraction as big the people would be dancing on the streets. Fortunately for dance, and ironically if you will, the painters are one source of patronage for choreographers. So are the composers. Advanced painters and composers like the new choreographers. They are the most elite audience the choreographers have. They know what's happening. They go to the concerts, they collaborate with the choreographers, and sometimes they make financial donations.

This column is not a statistical survey of benefits accruing to dancers. Most dancers are not starving. But I am implying that would-be choreographers are easily discouraged by a scene that offers little bread to keep the body going and little recognition to stir the ego. To begin with, there is hardly any frame of reference for an aspiring choreographer to guide his action through the maze of historical developments up to various contemporary attitudes and forms. A painter on his way to New York is already familiar with current styles through the writings and reproductions in countless coffee-table books on art, and in the national and international art magazines. If the painter is really curious, he knows all about the styles of the century, the preceding centuries, and the centuries before that. An informed painter is steeped in the history of his craft. Choreographers have to depend on a single national magazine, which is a disgrace to any literate dancer. Moreover, one photograph of a dance or dancer (unlike photos of painting) is not very informative; and descriptive-analytical writing that might illuminate a photo or series of photos is practically unknown. Art writing is sophisticated beyond belief compared to dance writing.

Choreographers need at least one major organ in the country to represent history in depth perspective, and current forms of depth analysis, both by the writers and by the choreographers themselves. I'm in favor of a constant resurrection of history in the interests of the future. Anyhow, the weight of history is always active in the present. The ignorance of dancers and public can't deter the inevitable presence of history in current activities. History is both contained in and transformed by the present. It is to the advantage of dancers and public to make history operative in a contemporary framework. Changes in contemporary forms depend upon historical revelations. History itself is in constant change as contemporary workers distort the far or immediate past to suit the needs of the time. History is remade at every stage of a continuous game. The improvement of communications in dance should lead to greater mobility in the assimilation and production of original work.

Informed publications are not the only source of information for public and artists. Gaudy, misinformed spreads in pulpy magazines can also inspire interest. Better than all magazines and papers put together would be a system of communications devolving upon movies. I can imagine a day when the public can buy documentary films to show at home the way people buy scores and records of contemporary music. Today, the films of dances are tucked away in archives or held by promoters for special theatre showings. In any event, there are very few movies of dances, and most of them are not documentary: they're artsy distortions based on film techniques rather than on the dances themselves.

When there's nothing to see there's nothing to talk about. When there's nothing to talk about everybody's in the dark. The people may come and go in the rooms, but they'll continue to talk about the pictures that are available to be seen.

ROBERT WHITMAN

1966-09-08

Robert Whitman presented a beautiful happening or theatre thing rather he would prefer maybe (to call it) in East Hampton August 27 and 28. The location was fantastic although I couldn't see it too well. It was a NIGHT TIME event. The location was fantastic. Whitman lit the place up for tripping the lights. I thought I was in a metaphorical paradise. I was. I couldn't find my seat, which was in a field. The field was full of grass and other weeds and there was also a swamp and nobody stepped on it (except the performers). But first of all (and last) I walked through an alley of paper bags glowing candles. They made a curving country path leading from the road where two guides (policemen) led the performing spectators with their flash, lights, down to three enormous plexiglass sheets sprayed with copper to make them into mirrors and situated so as to form a kind of room (enclosure). I found myself in the mirrors. I thought I was a clown at a country fair, or an amusement park. I was. Distortions are a riot if it doesn't bother you. From there I watched a number of other distortions, although I didn't get it at first. This is what happened: a young dancer named Deborah Hay stood or danced, in the room between the mirrors; actually she imitated (she told me) the kinds of distortions these mirrors make—by shifting her weight slowly from foot to foot and making other subtle gestures with her head, hands, shoulders etc., and at some moment she was reflected in herself by a young man who stood directly opposite her (body) and did or seemed to be trying to do exactly what she was doing. Meanwhile a number of children (and other people) were entering the boat tent, for real I mean the swamp-field, for the journey through this outer space Antarctica (later) and as they passed by Deborah between the three mirrors, we spectators by now enjoying ourselves on lovely blue pillows, sailing along as it were, I noticed these children—who were entering—reflected (like Deborah) on another big sheet or screen located directly in front of us. Whitman somehow connected (transmitted) these images from one place to another. It reminded me of closed circuit television where you look at yourself in store windows. It was great. Okay. Next. By this time I was so comfortable I didn't feel like moving but a gentlemanly neighbor suggested we pick our bodies up off our pillows and take a stroll to our right where events themselves in this boat of a happening theatre seemed to be moving. The water became more apparent. I saw myself reflected in it. After all it was a swamp. As we moved along I saw what I had already seen which is to say another large screen (in the trees) upon which (the screen) a naked lady was robing and disrobing. The other performers (spectators), or most of them, didn't move along with me and my neighbor. They must have liked the screen lady. The SKY was also voluptuous. It was night time. After the happening I mentioned to a friend that I thought the sky was El Greco (Toledo) that weekend and we agreed. But as for the happening itself: there were literally two more screens in the trees, moving always to the right as it were. On one of them I heard some sound, which was coming from a noise box situated someplace in the swamp. On the screen itself Whitman made a journey to Antarctica (mentioned earlier) utilizing icebergs, boats, penguins, and other paraphernalia that I'm having difficulty remembering since so much was going on all at once, including the crickets in the thickets. The noise box was transmitting a man's voice talking about what we were fortunate enough to be looking at on the screen. I liked the connection. It was almost osmotic. On the fourth and last (to the right) screen another film appeared but I couldn't make it out so I thought about it. A few children standing nearby, close to the water swamp, mentioned that this screen looked like a whale or a cloud or a balloon and I instantly (later) remembered Moby Dick, which to my surprise was not an original thought because one of the performers (Julie) told me it looked closer to a whale of a Moby pillow. Wow. Bemeantimes I was standing as far to the right as was possible (without keeling over) when along came about six penguins or girls in plastic bags sort of waddling by the grass. They then disappeared. Now I recall seeing (earlier) a number of phosphorescent figures at a great distance from our blue pillows who also retreated into the forest. June bugs. Lightning flies. The night was still clear and while I was noting various other phenomena in my trusty notebook I spied a tent (tabernacle) deep in the forest. I was beginning to think I should go there (the next stop on the right see) when a confident performer notified me that the lit up tent was actually a supply place for the theatre event and I could go there if I wanted for refreshments. I didn't. One of the last things I saw in this "metaphor" was another young dancer by name Tony Holder paddling about very relaxed in something in the reflected water—towing behind him an incredible white sculpture construction. I didn't mention all the colors in this event but I'm sure you can see for yourself. White stands for Moby. Soon I wandered back over my path to the left thinking a great deal about how nice it was to be there. The crickets were sounding off. So was a finale noise box interpreting the sounds of the swamp. Simone (Whitman) told me it was more truly the sound of paper crackling through the trees in the wind. At that point I couldn't have cared less.

P.S. Norman Brown is a genius. The revue could be transcribed as a parody of Brown. Synaptically speaking. If you saw something I didn't see, sorry. Oh one more thing: when Tony (Holder) was in his rowboat someone behind us tossed up firecrackers (maybe flashlights) which landed all around Tony especially for him to fish for. The noise was FANTASTIC. I guess Whitman is a genius too.

DANCING IS A DOG

1967-11-02

Remarks occasioned by a program at the New School called "Avant-Garde Forms and Sources":

Funny how you see a thing when it isn't there and when it's there you don't see it anymore. I don't clean my house but I polish my boots. Much of theatre occurs on the stage and much of it occurs in the heads of the audience. Dancing is a dwarf lady, Yvonne said once. Or dancing is a dog. Steve Paxton had a friendly dog on stage with him and they had this nice relationship. Somebody asked Steve how much of the dog's action was on cue and he said it wasn't that kind of relationship. Steve has a lot of dancing credentials. But he doesn't see it skillwise any more. His body isn't up for sale. (Economically, things get tougher.) He has a sort of casual friendly attitude about the business. Clasp your hands and there's the steeple, open the doors and see all the people. If the world's a stage nobody should mind showing off. Theatres are special gaping places, like monkey houses. At the Bronx Zoo in the ape section a wise joker played a neat switch with a mirror and a sign under it that says "you are looking at the most dangerous animal in the world." Well who did we come here to look at anyway? So sometimes an audience gets to look at itself. The Pied Piper hands out a bunch of cards with silly word cues on them. They function like a mirror. Certainly the stage is invisible. Once I remember Steve did a dance in which he snapped pictures of the audience. Another guessing game about who's who in anybody's arena. Walk out of the house and you're on, baby. The cards had name cues on them. Call out a name, a body responds and reads a line on the card. "Margy" and "Leon" stole the show for a while. Margy kept standing up on her seat to acknowledge herself. Finally she and Leon jumped into the aisle and hugged each other. Dancing is also disregarding instructions. Thou shalt break the rules to play the game with maximum satisfaction. Like even the low wit of mixing sexes. Some girl said she was David, another insisted she was George, and a guy said yeah he was Liz. Everyone was thrilled. Audiences are good to themselves.

Gus Solomons, Jr., also gave them a whack at it, but he didn't hand it over. Audience participation they call it. I think that's a slimy expression but maybe it says something about the state of the nation. Gus alternated speaking into a mike and dancing a few set movement sequences. At the mike he encouraged people to "make noise or ask questions during the piece" because "if you make noise while I'm moving it will affect your impression" and "one way to understand is to participate" and "one way to understand is to ask questions." So there were noises and questions. Curiosity about the performer. Where is your abdomen? Why does he want to know where your abdomen is? Do you like what you're doing? Why don't you answer the questions? Gus concluded by asking, "Frankly, are there any answers?" An academic question. The form of the piece is partly a question. Answers are fatal to the entertainment of questions.

Dancing is questionable. Dancing is sometimes not being here. Can you know what a thing is without knowing what it isn't? The form of Kenneth King's piece was his absence. He set it up as a hoax: a phony letter about being in Hong Kong and a brief appearance before the concert began (walking in front of the curtain) in an outfit only people who know him would recognize him in. Absent with true regrets was Yvonne Rainer. Dancing is information about an illness enforcing absence. A tape recording of a technical letter from doctor to doctor on the nature of a frightful intestinal condition. We wish a speedy recovery. Probably it's a poor joke to suggest that dancing might be a "blind loop syndrome involving a defunctionalized colon." Yvonne was represented on the program by what she does best, in this case a section called "Mat" from "The Mind Is a Muscle" performed by William Davis and Becky Arnold. Mildly gymnastic and stuntlike, changes of position without stopping, no confrontation with the audience, an uninflected dynamic, a continuum of movement with no apparent beginning or ending, very smooth and relaxed, as much not there as there—it's hard to imagine a dancing dance less like dancing than this sort of dance. It's impressive to be so unimpressed.

CANCELLED

1967-11-30

Fun City is picking up. I must congratulate Elaine Sturtevant on her revival of Satie's "Relâche." It was a total success. A cancelation can't go wrong. Things are always going wrong. Absence is perfection. "Thou ceaseth to be something thou hadst done better never to become." Life is a rain check to oblivion. If we could earn a living on cancelations we might forget ourselves when we leave the house and go straight to the sandbox. "Relâche" does mean "suspension of performance." I refused to look it up in the dictionary before going to the theatre. Someone told me there would be a performance. Someone else said there wouldn't. Rumors of Elaine and Bob Rauschenberg appearing naked. Rumors of omission. A friend said he wouldn't miss what Elaine does because she comes to his things. "But you'd better look it up in the dictionary before we go, Jill." In "The Banquet Years" Shattuck says that "Relâche" was scheduled on a Thursday in November, 1924, and the people found the theatre tight shut. A week later there was a performance. Both evenings were scandalous.

There was no scandal Monday night, November 20, at the School of Visual Arts. Westchester might find it disgraceful but not the people I know, for whom scandal is a way of life. Well—a few of us in the lounge were mildly enjoying the joke and the good company. Niceties all around: "That's what you get for having a smattering of French." Or, "How long shall we stay to experience the cancelation?" We exit and appreciate the fine lettered poster pasted on the door: "Sturtevant–Relâche." Two people get out of a taxi and approach the door. It's Marcel Duchamp and his wife. We have a few words. Yes there's no performance. Yes "Relâche" means cancelation. Yes he appeared nude in the original production. They've kept the taxi waiting. I watch his diminutive figure retreat in the night. Beautiful. Wouldn't have missed it for anything. From Paris to

New York and forty-three years in between. Nothing is deleted. That which is deleted has always existed. Whatever is is constantly in deletion. Existence and deletion the same thing.

Cancelation art: demonstration of the void in the thing and the thing in the void. Also a demonstration of subjective continuity. Monuments in the mind. Easy come easy go. In Chicago a home for the elderly is being built on the site of the landmark of the garage where the St. Valentine's Day gangland massacre took place in 1929. Last Thursday, November 16, James Byars, itinerant artist of the world, paper expert, commuter to Japan, laid out a 500-foot paper man on Fifty-third Street between Fifth and Sixth Avenues. Fifty St. Thomas Choir School boys stretched out flat along the edges of the man to hold him down. The head was at the Modern Museum, the crotch at the Craft Museum, the feet at the CBS Building. Flusher trucks from the Garbage Department moved in with 20,000 gallons of water. They slid and skid, confounded by a sheet of paper. It took 100 hours to make and 10 minutes to destroy. The exhibit ended at noon exactly. The Donnell Library was playing a movie: "No Reason to Stay." The half-mile of paper was furnished by Gilreth International Company which makes this dissolvable paper—a recent biochemical discovery. Spy paper. It's a sterile edible material. Spies can now eat their information. A fat man in a gray flannel suit protested the papershow by tearing up his New York Times. "This paper has undone me."—"Shut your mouth dame or with this paper shall I stop it." (Shakespeare)

CULTURAL GANGSTERS

1968-06-06

To whom it may concern: Pardon me Jill or Okay Fred or Thanks Diane. Yours sincerely. It's all the same to me Alphonse. Really the incest in the world is frightening. I was on a very incestuous panel last week. We'd been making love to each other for so long I felt I had to invent a disagreement here and there to make it look good. (Someone noted that half the panel was or is married to the moderator). Not that lovers don't quarrel on occasion but when the lovers meet in public they present a united front and it comes over quite cozy. I'm still mystified by the function of a panel discussion. Perhaps it's just another community get-together. That sounds vague enough to make it seem both essential and unnecessary. If the idea is to be instructive I don't believe in it. Nobody wants to be instructed. I think they come to see the famous people (har). I picked out the famous people in the audience (my friends) and felt more and more incestuous about it. In fact I began to think if things went right we could've had a gang bang on the spot without even knowing it. Possibly we did. Okay now I'm gonna be serious (not that I wasn't). I think the panel was every bit as world-shaking as that thing I read about where those cultural gangsters Mailer, Schlesinger, and Marcuse got together to straighten out democracy. They didn't have a Gene Swenson at their thing. Gene is a very disruptive guy but I'll tell you I was at a party once where Mailer and another guest were beating each other into a bloody pulp, and Gene is basically a harmless democrat with excellent vocal projection. He could improve his style but what he's doing is actively creating the kind of impossible situation that reduces all that talking to zero. Are you cats ready to plug your audio into the electric-circuit sound system? No we weren't. Frankly my sympathies were divided between Gene and my commitment to the panel protocol. One question might be how to make a lover out of Gene. We could've accepted the tootsie rolls he offered us in the beginning. But by some absurd reasoning, to embrace Gene would be to deprive him of his outrageous function. By another twist, to acknowledge Gene this way or that way outside the etiquette of the panel would be to subvert our own function. But then you might ask—what happens to the etiquettes when the people start storming the Bastille (by that time I hope to be squatting by the seashore mindlessly under the sun upon my knees in the sand). So at some level the panel was Gene the people raging against the authority of us the government. (Do not go gentle into that good night.) That Gene was ejected finally was the power of the law. Since I'm a minor criminal myself I felt uncomfortable about suddenly being on the side of the law. I would have objected if I hadn't been deadlocked as I said by my divided sympathies. When Gene was up there on the balcony screaming quotes from Mao or Ho Chi shortly before ejection Yvonne was sputtering to me to do something because I'd promised I could "handle it" but I thought it was handling itself. I mean it was just another happening. Assuming authority is one kind of occupational hazard and Gene knows the price he can pay for being an uninvited bully. Artistically, we were a combine of two simultaneous events not brought together by single design. Audience participation in the form of questions from the floor belonged to our event in the accepted protocol of a panel. Another exception was a muted expression of Gene's vocal apoplexy. For a few minutes a young man quietly made his way through rows of audience members. Later he asked us what we thought of his performance. Meredith Monk said she liked it and I said I liked it too, that he was wearing a nice maroon sweater and a pleasant beard (moustache). Simone Whitman thought it was uninspired and unimaginative. (When does the government accept the people as inspired?) I might have added he neatly illustrated an issue posed by the panel. The title of the panel was "Dance and Its Alternatives." Robert Morris, the moderator, said he devised the title and that it wasn't especially relevant. I thought it was. Actually Morris disposed of it at the outset by defining it historically as the cleavage between dance traditionally based on studio techniques with concomitant "performing" attitudes, and dance reconsidered as a response to tasks, rule-games, objects, and the like. I thought of it also in a broader sense of an "alternative" being an attitude about dance as a constant activity in the world whether it's framed in a box or wandering on the streets. I suggested that if a groovy president proclaimed holidays like "tomorrow everybody will be dancing" eventually the population might think of themselves as dancers and so what. My panel companions have a greater vested interest in dance framed by a box to be viewed by invitation only (I could always be a "street critic") but they're completely hip to the nonsense of both the box thing and the street thing and I feel confident that as artists they'll continue to provoke controversy in their funambulism over the confusion of streets and boxes.

Meredith and Yvonne discussed a very interesting subject of static dancing and imagery. Like the difference between Yvonne dancing as static in its repetitiveness and uninflected energy dynamic, and Meredith's "still" images as static in a more conventional sense. I liked Meredith's explanation of a recent event in her loft which consisted in part of performers in repose located within open white boxes, cubes, rooms (or what)—the sculpture of Julias Tobias. She said she was reversing the usual situation of a static audience and mobile performers. This reversal in one aspect or another is the beautiful controversy of the times. I'm quite happy about the confusion if it doesn't result in mutual extinction. The inflammable issue of audience interference is one vital aspect of the whole mess. And once an audience is mobilized how do they know where the artist's work ends and theirs begins or vice versa. How does the artist know? At last, who is the artist?

Possibly the discussion of training and body types was also relevant. How do you accept or deal with fat, ugly, knock-kneed, or involuntary tics. Steve Paxton's democratic people concert was commended or questioned as an example of sympathetic toleration of a variety of types as performance material. I quoted a story I heard about someone who wasn't eligible for the Cunningham company because her ass was too big. Simone was talking about being in shape or out of shape—an occupational disease of dancers. I wanted to know how it was possible to be either in shape or out of shape being as how a shape is a shape. Yvonne was talking about her need for exercise and I quoted another story about an organization in California called "Athletes Anonymous" where, say, if one member is seized by an urge to play eighteen holes of golf he'll call another member who hastens over with a fifth of whiskey. One member said whenever he had the impulse to exercise he'd lie flat on his back on the floor until the impulse passed away. Sounds like an interesting dance. I just received a letter by the way from John Perreault. It says: "Jill Johnston plays in the sandbox; I play in the sand." Lucky bastard!

UNTITLED

1968-10-10

Somebody I know can't stand reading a thing like Norman Brown's "Love's Body" where "everything means everything else." Someone just told me about people who go to the trouble of tracing back their genealogy and find everybody in it, or a broken link that's unaccountable. All those skeletons in the closet. Every genealogy is a fiction. There's no such thing. There's only one genealogy. It takes place in our dreams. Every specific genealogy is a fiction. I just reread "Moses and Monotheism." I like it that a Jew such as Freud should have put himself out so much as to prove that Moses was an Egyptian. But everyone knows that Moses was a Mexican immigrant. And Malcolm X said Jesus was a black man. And they still don't know who Shakespeare was. I think he was an American

Indian posing as King James. For myself, I had three fathers and they were all illustrious. Moreover, my mother's three fathers and mine were one and the same, further elaborating the incestuous project. Anyhow, try figuring out your origins some balmy night on hash and saki or the likes. How many of those flying carpets have taken to the air in the course of luminous Oriental nights? Where were we when we last met? It must have been a memorable occasion.

I had a brief conversation with Diane, my editor, which in some corporate board meeting might have added up to a momentous decision. Actually it was a simple agreement. We agreed that a new column in these pages headed "Intermedia" or "Cross-over" would be an absurdity compounding an already absurd situation of medium categories which are becoming increasingly difficult to contain and define, much to my delight. This column is itself a joke. Any other name for it would be equally amusing. My model is the title of that ridiculous book by Havelock Ellis—"The Dance of Life." No doubt I'm saying the already obvious. What does it mean to name something? Where do we come off giving everything a legal identity? The genealogy of language is the same as for persons. It ends up in the paramecium, one of the most illegal of organisms. What do we do with language after accepting it as a practical expedient? In a real or pseudo-etymological exercise you can uncover the hoax of a frozen legal identity which finds its way into that mausoleum called the dictionary. The dictionary is the language equivalent of the doomsday book. Yet it's one of my favorite books. I use it all the time. I use it for work and for pleasure. It's utterly confusing. You can get a terrific high on the dictionary. What does it mean to encircle something and paste a name on it and qualify the name with adjectives born in somebody's hysterical manifesto and then say well now that it has a name and it means this and that it's all over baby. We're dead as soon as we're born with a name. We make ourselves new again by changing our names, by dreaming ourselves back into our real or pseudo genealogies. Or we make ourselves new not by changing the name but by repeating and repeating it into a magical transcendence of itself. It becomes meaningless by becoming so much itself.

This is a complex subject. I want to be clear and obtuse about it at the same time. The occasion is an orgy of poetry and intermedia thinking generated by three Poetry Events in Central Park, September 27–29, organized by John Giorno; followed by a heady discussion with John Perreault, who contributed one of the events. Perreault re-states the ancient purpose of poetry, all art. "Poetry breaks up the ordinary use of language to let more reality come through." Until recently poetry was never traditionally just naming things (excepting the primitives). Traditionally our Western poetry has made language new by altering the context of words within a grammatically correct syntax. In the recent tradition (Dada, Surrealism, Symbolism, etc.) the context of words was radically altered by the shattering of the conventional syntax. E.E. Cummings, for instance. Syntax is linear. Its breakup is a collusive synthesis. Poets and artists had been doing this a long time before McLuhan delivered it to an unsuspecting public. Intermedia is the ultimate realization of a synthesis that's been taking place all century in each medium. Cubism was one of the first radical manifestations of it in painting. Prophets of the new intermedia are the likes of Cage, Artaud, and Schwitters, to name three if I must. Each medium is now transcending itself by emphasizing or extending each aspect of itself which relates to every other extension of our senses. The traditional legalized medium (i.e. painting) projects the stimuli for one of our senses as supreme. Environmental sculpture, painting, etc., is one sort of intermedia attempt to put the object back in the forest where it's a tree among trees. In the forest every sense is equally supreme.

The artists are making a last-ditch stand to re-integrate what the child and the savage do naturally. Words are pictures are sounds are sights are touch are smell are the altogether forever. The artists are rampaging through the graveyards of the file cabinets to throw the alphabetized cards into the beautiful chaos of the altogether from whence they were so painfully extracted to make a mess called civilization.

Intermedia is as old as the hills, as Emmett Williams said of the new kind of picture poem called Concrete Poetry. Our oldest ancestors were the great intermedia people. The new intermedia developments are not an indication of progress but of regression. To regress is to progress. If there's such a thing as progress it means to go back. To find again the child and the savage in us. To cure ourselves by finding again the all at once altogether. By naming things we separated things. By naming things in logical syntax we separated the subject, verb, and object—the actor, the action, and that which is acted upon. Somehow it came about that even artists, among the best of children in a childless society, called themselves poets or composers or dancers or painters or sculptors. The new synthesis is a hallucination and McLuhan rightly pointed out that the opening of all our senses to all the data would result in hallucination.

Perreault dates the recent intermedia activity of poets from 1965. He says he himself took courage from John Giorno who at that time was beginning to put his "found" poems on tape and project them in an environmental situation of black light. Giorno was inspired by William Burroughs and Brion Gyson. Perhaps the only poet whom people identify as a poet who was earlier pushing the performance aspect of poetry into a deeper extension of itself was Jackson Maclow. Jackson was the only poet, considered a poet in the formal sense, associated with the Fluxus exploration of the late fifties and early sixties in which everybody was everything. If you asked me what George Brecht is today I couldn't tell you. If you say artist, people think painter, etc. The last time somebody asked me what I did I said I was an archaeologist. Having said it I believe it. A jolly new profession. They asked me then if I'd done any exciting digging lately and I said yes absolutely all the time. I think the guy who dug up Troy was one of my ancestors. But about Jackson. He was one of the poets in the Central Park evenings. With the exception of slides projected on the back wall of the bandshell he was doing what he's been doing for a decade or more, in this case: a poem made by chance (he too was a student in Cage's 1957 course at the New School) and delivered by a chorus of five as a superimposed overlapping etc. simultaneous exposition of a simple story about "the turtles embark upon a journey to the sea whose course is a mystery ... no one knows where the turtle goes ..." The text is both chanted and spoken. The story is heard in fragments as well as in a syntactical sentence.

As a poet connected with and emerging from the New York School of Poets (led by the older Ashbery, Koch, O'Hara) Perreault had no tradition for moving into a performance situation beyond a straight reading. His friends in fact initially opposed the move. The New York School of course overlaps with the beat poets (Ginsberg, Corso, Ferlinghetti, Burroughs) and the Black Mountain School of Olson, Creeley, Duncan, et. al. With perhaps an exception here and there, including the well-known disrobings (Ginsberg) in the fifties, the readings were always straight podium deliveries. Excepting a fiery prophets like Ginsberg, Perreault thinks they're all a great bore, the readings. He says that if the standard device of poetry is to involve all the senses through words by suggestion, the next logical step is to actually do it. As a poet turned performer, in the broadest sense, he's involved in the making of a new tradition in his medium, at the moment shared by Giorno, Maclow, Anne Waldman, Michael Benedikt, Hannah Weiner, Emmett Williams (all on the Central Park events), and probably others I don't know about or slipping my mind. As such they merge with all the other artists whose particular mediums (a habit they can't or don't want to shake) may appear to remain the paramount aspect of an intermedia situation but whose concerns are expressing the great longing and project of an era running short on survival time.

Re-integration. The everything as everything. The organism as totally illegal. The legality of nothing but pleasure in an orgy of self-reproduction (the paramecium). The end of importance. The end of politics. The end of hierarchies. The end of families. The end of groups. The end of the earth as a penal colony (Burroughs).—No end to what there can be an end of in the great re-integration: the intermedia of the cosmic village; the intermedia of the genealogy as a vast prolific dream;

the intermedia of language as the gurgling of happy infants; the intermedia of hordes of artists (all the people) making sand castles and other important inanities inside and outside their heads, or doing nothing at all. Intermedia is the world before and after we chop it up into bits of pieces and stash it away in a filing cabinet labeled MINE, YOURS, THEIRS.

I'll have to continue this next week. I want to say a few concrete things about the actual performances, including observations about the language itself, in part inspired by the discussions with Perreault.

Meanwhile, off the subject (or on I think) I wish to add my salute to those of my friends (and everybody) to Marcel Duchamp whom I have often saluted and met only twice and talked with just once. He has always lived and will continue to live. He made us and he was everything we made him. He was made long before and ahead of his time. We should be happy.

LETTERS FROM CAMP

1969-05-01

April 23rd: Being stabilized a few days to meet the gravediggers I'm in a position to report that Bridget Polk thinks for out-loud reading my writing needs a few more periods. She told me this the night of April 23rd. She said she read my piece to Andy by phone since he'd heard I was writing away about Viva again, therefore what was it, so Bridget gave an oral recitation she says and I'm paraphrasing it was hard on her breathing. April 23rd was lavender letter day. I made notes on it even. More than five. For point six I'm sending Pete Hamill a poisonal engraved invitation to that panel. The incest in the world is getting worse. I had a prolonged conversation for the first time in 10 years with my superior editor Dan Wolf, by phone, and this happened April 23rd also. Moreover, Danny Moses of Simon & Schuster who is now as of that day another superior approximately 4 p.m. it happened I'm talking about the same day, it's crocking my mind, this finalized an awful lot of officializing a red tape worm into my present weak stomach condition over several months, resulting from a single sentence written by Danny one day in response I think to a sex column I wrote, the one about me and Polly out at George Segal's farm posing naked (George is showing it May 1st he says the same day as Ann's Bowery Show, and he put hair on me not on Polly which might be pretty hip, George must be moving into the aesthetics of sex differentiation), Danny as the sentence began told me in the bar of the Time-Life building where I had to sign up, that April 23rd was not only Shakespeare's birthday, but the day he died as well. I was appalled. I'm not accustomed to such candid connections. For instance a little girl last week told me that if you ever see a horse with bosoms you'll know it's Lois Lane. Further, in reference to "Star" showing Julie Andrews that "men should be in a different bus because the ladies wouldn't wanna be disgusted." I have to complete the story. This column was originally meant to concern the holy trinity of sex fame and money. On April 23rd or the day before I happened to be wearing Ted Webster's shirt, I like wearing other people's things, in the morning, and he called out of the blue he made it back from Korea apparently, when in the evening of the following day I casually mentioned that story about Martin Luther having his vision on a toilet and Ted agreed money is shit but it has possibilities. Or I should put it into a questionable formulation, an old cliche: Can you buy love as well as sex with money and if not why so and if so why not be famous in order to be locked up behind a fortress to recall the good old days of your anonymity when you bought your money with your sex or vice versa. Anyhow, about that little girl, she also told me she wanted a penis. She's not nearly as advanced as my daughter. By that time I was upset and disgusted and she was throwing some lousy old marshmallows at me and pretending to be a baby etcetera but I took hold of myself and consoled her by saying listen you've got something on the inside and something on the outside and you should be so lucky and later on if you're a nice girl you'll have additional problems. I didn't ask her why Lois Lane is now a centaur. The comic books are getting very informative. A mother was complaining about it. I think the kids know best. Besides all this, the night of April 23rd at a party my friend Ann Wilson gave me thanks a lot Ann it was great actually it was a celebration a success scandale my coming out party etc., Bridget Polk had along her cock book, too many cocks I said, but a beautiful book, she showed me one page of Andy a head thereof and a trunk or a cylinder or what in brown coloring leading down with the head into Sonny Liston's portrait, two or three more heads, of Sonny, Bridget said that was the balls to the rest of the cock meaning I guess the trunk the cylinder the torso topped by Andy the head and then on top of that not whip cream but a typeset print collage a line reading, "Now I'm so famous I can walk down the street with Jill Johnston." Oh wow listen I said who said that. She said Andy said it so I said I dunno I better quit writing again like Gregory keeps saying publicly me more private I do it I can't stop I'll go on a binge if this keeps up. But regardless Ann Wilson then said the nicest thing to me about how I pulled a Virginia Woolf act by I think, I was embarrassed so I didn't find out for sure, by saying and I'm quoting myself now, "that's the ultimate compliment Bridget coming from Ann because she (Ann) has been making those books for 20 years." It's true. Ann is a great artist. I think Bridget is now too, I never saw so many cocks in one night. I wonder if there's any sex or money or power involved. But this column is about April 23rd. Danny (Moses) gave me another good line after signing my life away on the 40th floor. John Quinn helping out was with us too. John, who earlier, or later, discussed the economy of emotions, I mean how you have always the same amount of money whether you're spending more or less it doesn't matter since they say I have no money at all now but I say look I had no money at all before and now I'm richer right and John emphasized the fact that anybody's economy is dependent upon their emotions and

I agree. It's all in the mind. It just looks different. Change the subject. No I forgot what Danny said, see above. I'll solve this sentence solution yet. Danny said, according to John, I never sign anything anybody gives me. That's what I said. Right. Then Danny replied, we've got it crooked now, "I'll bet you never sign a petition." For that compliment I gave him "Black Elk speaks." He's very learned so I didn't know what's best. To my agentress I donated "Love's Body" which she might've read also. And I keep stressing all this happened in one day. Another coincidence was that Ted came into New York from Korea the day The Voice came out my column saying something about the poor guy and I told 'im never mind I didn't mention your name. Also that very night, the same 23rd after Ann's party at Max's, after Bridget said David Bourdon must be in love with me, and I said uh uh Bridget he's in love with you, and after another cocked-up story about how she wrote to the Pope asking for a drawing of St. Peter's dome because she was crippled and would never be able to get there and she collects religious drawings, she had a congenital disease; after all this news me lads and me dames we're at Max's quite flaked out we see Viva who donates a g-string a beautiful silver affair wouldn't go around your thumb to David who doesn't need it I said I steal it right away put it in my boot lose it retrieve it etc.—whatta collector's item! Further on thank Peter she's happily married. I dig her husband. He looks like her. They're going to Rome. Or to home. To bed anyhow. I don't think they bought each other. Y'never know. According to anybody's calculations for the 1970s re the space landing the birth of the rocket is the Death of Christianity. Or as Polly says we don't know what to do with a phallus so we send it into outer space. They might even have a Bowery Savings Bank on the Moon. By phone Guillaume got another anonymous message. They assured me the travelling was fine. I said yeah natch especially when you can write home about it, letters to mommie from camp. My superior editors will take care of the messages from home. Gregory and a Cyril Nelson from Dutton are also as of April 23rd, I signed up with them too alas, on my side. My trust in the gods is a blessing to nobody if you can't be French. Here's the final serious sentence: Ann asked who wrote about Gauloise cigarettes at the party. David said Robbe-Grillet. Bridget says big cucumbers are the rule at the Holy Cross Mission. I say I stole a bottle of French wine from a lady thought I was a servant so I misbetrusted myself unto her highness. I say as well, continuing the academic line from last week, that the incest in England is outrageous, that in 1776 the collective European sons fought the collective European fathers and so on or as Gene Swenson succinctly put it once ages ago the American Revolution of 1776 succeeded because the defenders of tradition liked rubbing their noses into the shit of the King, and all the King's horses and all the King's shit that he was willing to spare wasn't enough to preserve their habits. I'm not sure what that means and I never agree with Gene politically but I think Gene is a great writer and for that reason I stuck it in. And too why I'm getting a French passport next time around for another unholy alliance because and this is really serious along with the space landings in the '70s, according to another Gemini waiter I talked to in a restaurant, we agreed, the French the British the Americans will arrive at a spiritual entente never mind the initials NEA NOB or SOB or what all those organizations and this will occur since the word guilt is no longer applicable to modern living. The guilt over the revolution, the Indians notwithstanding, is now a bloody bore of a drag in the Civil War too if you want to I don't.

THE BELLES IN THE TOWERS

1969-05-22

Many children call the blocks towers if they happen to build them upward, which they usually do since space is at a premium on the school desk strewn with this kind of material. Ann reminds me the Hunchback of Notre Dame died in the Tower. Beyond that she says the end of her own novel was going to be just tower after tower, every kind of tower she could lay her hands on. Specific graphic descriptions. My own diagrams involve a quadrangle centered by a lily pool bounded by the brick walls of two stories of corridors supporting two castellated towers rising above a mountain top overlooking a river. Stan Van Der Beek says the Empire State Building was built with 200 tons of extra structural steel to prevent it from swaying so dirigibles could be moored to the top of it now realized in a modern concession to common sense by a Pan Am flight from a float roof to a landing strip or vice versa from passport to heliocopter. Whereas his wife Johanna has dreamt that she was interested in her husband's tower in which dream he replied that he needed it to throw his weight around at the time. They had to conserve their energy for a future purpose. The twin towers are united by a garland of flowers arcing from spire to spire. The staircase winds upward into a discovery of the unity in circles, for circularity is the common principle which characterizes all instances that can be called circular. I rush down the staircase anyhow and yell at the top of my lungs. The metal echoes the clang of an ancient boot. I carry a small wooden weight to carry on its chain the three keys to the locks leading into a tower of bells made in 1931 by Gillet and Johnston in Croydon, England. Later it was converted from a foundry into a munitions factory. Johanna says that someplace in New York an iron foundry was converted to buttons for Civil War uniforms. On two sides of the lower part of the tower were cut the first verse of Psalm 127 in the Vulgate. The bells number 30. In 1932 Thomas Hayes Proctor went to the top of the Notre Dame Cathedral with his wife Edith who was paralyzed by the accelerating volume of the biggest bell ringing the noon hour by the weight of a man falling onto a board extending from the bell to make the clapper bong against the insides of its metal supported by a wooden structure including an iron ring for the bell man to hold in his efforts to notify the country of its time. Tom says Edith was paralyzed she couldn't move at all he tried to get her down but afterward she made her first acquaintance with Vouvray wine on the Boulevard. Tom is 84. Edith is gone. He lives with his sister Hilda. He gives me a book of essays about Whitehead inscribing the book to Jill with affection and with contrition for having inoculated her with the virus of philosophy, a disease from which she has never recovered. But I'm into psychology now Tom. And he says the power of God is the worship he inspires. And I say it's the separation of mind and body what created our civilized illnesses. And he says not nearly as much as the identification of the mind and the body and I'm thinking o phooey it isn't a notion but a fact, since he's going on beautifully as usual, the same old lucidity, stringing garlands from Plato to Whitehead, the twin gods, the notion of union as a complexity reducing all differences to non entity and discovering ways of unifying factors in differences which to him is Plato's great contribution to philosophy, yet he makes me promise to send it back to him, a paper he wrote 1938, swearing I can only borrow it on my heart on whatever organ I consider most sacred. He waits in the car while I go up in the tower. He doesn't know who made them. How come if he taught there for about 35 years. He says his memory is fading. It isn't, but he cares more about the cello than the bells. Also he says he's learning a lot from reading "Sappho's Daughters." You can't keep it though Tom and I try to give him another such book in the pornie line for the type he represents. But he wants to know the latest. He thinks it must be anatomically impossible to get two vaginas together. I'm inside the tower. We can be sure that if we put all the necessary mathematical bricks in front of them they will not only build their mathematics out of wooden bricks but build a truly abstract and yet personal mathematics in their minds out of the mental bricks they have fashioned for themselves during the play. I can't wait to see the bells but I won't. Can we look at the internal structure of what we have to divide? Is a tower in the middle of a modern city called a skyscraper for anybody to be impaled on its spire? Am I opening the right doors to the kingdom of the keys? Is the possibility of an indefinite continuation of the process perhaps the first door opening towards the concept of infinity which they say the children find extremely exciting? I dunno. If the tower seldom falls in one piece and it breaks in two before it hits the ground because the part near the bottom is anxious to get there according to the principle that the taller it gets the bigger the base and the top will undo itself to crush and crumble down onto its bottom not being able to support its erected member I'm inside a structure that isn't working out as to its share of blocks which were the only ones left on my desk in any case, as an answer to the problem. So I dream as I did in 1965 I fly up against the roof of a vault and fall down into a coma from which I recover by awakening to discover my fist. Johanna says I'll never impress anybody ever again with my special abilities. And they used to watch me. I was the only one who could do it. But I don't care what they say anymore about saying it out loud, snickering as though Freud was the first who said it and you haven't read about it yourself. I can fly if I have a mind to. You lie down flat on your back all dead. You decide to fly so you tense up your stomach muscles and erect into a sitting position by straining at the neck and so on. Then you stand up. Then you take off. You flap the appendages called the arms by beating them against your breasts and yelling Tarzan or Jane and grabbing a handy rope and swinging from bell to balcony to rescue a princess from a big bad witch. Ann says the bell in the tower is like the virgin in the garden or the architectural structure of the cloisters is based upon the medieval symbolism of the virgin as an unviolated woman in a garden of that description. But according to my diagram the cloisters forms only one side of a quadrangle centered by a lily pool bounded by a courtyard enclosed by four walls of bricks enduring the birds in the singing vines away under the castellated towers rising above two arches known as sally ports trough which you could walk or even drive a car into the courtyard bounded on one side by the cloisters a long narrow corridor where we kept the winter sleds. The French windows rattled from the sounds of the train below the mountain. The belles in the towers were the girls on our way to be burned by the sun in the spring of a sky blue year. I was a female Icarus in that dream I say and I'm complaining I can't appreciate the sensation of a melting arm. Not unless I'm ready to go to sleep. And I'm thinking damn damn where's the keys? O Judas Iscariot and all the priests I can't get out, or in. They're locking me in. The sheep are climbing out of the ground. The steps are spiraling into a dizzy spell. I can't breathe. I've got claustrophobia bad. My palms are clammy. From reading the information on the walls. From stealing a picture and stuffing it into my pocketbook. From climbing when I should be resting. I'm into a panic.

IN HER ALTOGETHER ALSO

1970-01-29

She stood up from a hot tub and passed out under the sink and broke a rib or two. I like to fall asleep myself in the middle of a story. Come again when you can't stay so long. And bring camera. My blood is thin, my heart is made of tin tonight. I didn't remember signaling with my foot my intention of dying with her and my foot isn't even stuck in the door. I'm stuck on the hi-way. Clapping my hands I am not singing joyfully in the moonlight. Frigid cold out as witches' tits.

I stopped because of an interesting noise. Flapflapflapflap ... Slowing down it goes flap-flap-flap. Get out inspect the rear parts. It isn't the dislodged metal thing or any other hanging thing, it's a hunk of rubber on the wheel detaching itself from the parent body, so I stand some special helpless looking slouch leaning longingly in the direction of oncoming vehicles my Havid scarf arranged at some attractive chest spread. Wish the photographer was here. Whiz whiz. Nada nobody. Whiz whiz. Bastids. If I were dead praps all the problems that bothered her would be settled. What was the great catastrophe before the drying up of the oceans? The coming of the snows. I should be pacing back and forth looking like I have an appointment at the end of the world. Last year this time according to a Voice office index card I was "envolved in many strange and wondrous adventures ...." I should be leaning on my car watching a bright red sports number slow down a few yards in front of my hood. Two smiling muscle boys are walking toward me, I hunch into my scarf and meet them halfway and stare at the snow and mumble about a disintegrating tire. Ye-s-s. And as they're into the jack and spare boy scout act I'm noting their Massachusetts license plate. It reads SOS. Terrific. I've been saved. I love being saved. Maybe while she was standing up from the hot tub and passing out under the sink I was backing into a snow bank stuck solid and gaily hacking away at the white stuff with a dust pan in order to find my way back to "grandmother's house" under the nothing night no stars even and falling into the embankments leaving the vehicle to be hauled out by the various rescue operation teams. I need photos of this business. No, I'm telling her, I'm not hiding my forehead, I'm showing my bangs. So she's clicking some pix of my bangs and other parts inside and outside but the "... strange and wondrous adventures" are not being recorded. Like looking out this window and seeing some abominable bird tracks and this leaning tower of silo and this deadduck apple orchard and many obscure but timeless traces of the great catastrophes before and after the drying up of the oceans. At that time according to certain prominent bioanalysts I became a female because another much stronger animal *also* anxious to return to the aquatic existence of which we had been deprived managed to bore a tube into me in order to create a passage to get into the puddle which became my uterus. Amazing. And I don't even have any callosities on my forward extremities to facilitate the clasping of any other weakling who got bored into. But I'm sitting in my vest and shirt and pants and pipe at the table looking at a chess set opposite my opponent in her altogether also staring at the chess pieces about level with a pair of great knockers before the separation of creation from nothing there was probably something. Flap. I'm leaning on my elbow describing a checkmate. This was my brilliant dephallible idea to get a shot like the original Duchamp at chess with the chick in the buff a blubber possibly detaching itself from the parent bodily situation to which the organization of the female accommodated itself apropobly. I make a move. Assault with the intent to ravish. The set belonged to the master and his widow themselves. She loaned me the set. She didn't want me to make the picture. You don't play chess, she said. It doesn't matter, I play lots of games. My opponent's hair is black like the original but five inches longer and it's covering the profile. I don't care for my own. No, I'm showing my bangs. My blood is thick, my heart is made of doodlebugs tonight. If she were dead praps all the problems that didn't bother me would be unsettled. Let's shoot this one out in the snow she said. Yeah let's do it on the way to the road. Now sit in the chair. Now stand on the table. Now the hands. The bangs. The tie. The dingle dangle. Now take off your clothes. No I don't do that. "He looked at my naked body and found that it was perfect and therefore destroyed his sketches." There's no padding interposed any more between life and the world. This is not a strange and wondrous adventure. I'm not terrible enough to be beautiful and I'm not a streaming pillar of orange wax as a girl in a tangerine dress rising up out of a hot tub and melting away under the sink and I don't have an appointment at the end of the world. Either. Where's the SOS car? She said she was available, she'd never leave me, she has a beautiful soul too, and she's very good with crazy people and how could I resist her. Come again when you can't stay forever. I find myself suddenly within the Unthinkable Itself. The lens is two yards away. Jesus she's foreshortening some part of my bare extremities and possibly even boring another tube into me somewhere and I don't need another puddle or any other substitution for somebody else's aquatic existence. But it's dramatically decadent. Capote on the couch. Just one frame, for her she said. Sure, one frame. Then let's do it on the way to the road. Then let's go up in that leaning tower of silo and make some abominable bird tracks and find our way back to grandmother's house under the nothing night no stars even and break a rib or two and wait for the SOS boys and the cameras to each infinitely small thing is as large as large things can be isn't it grand?

"OF THIS PURE BUT IRREGULAR PASSION"

1970-07-02

In support of the gay movement on the occasion of the gay celebration week: I guess yes I've been saying it in this column for a year and a half now, but always fragmentarily in the context of the literary exercises. So this will be straight on. I don't recall any decision to declare my sexuality, in print, as though it should necessarily have interested anybody in any case. It happened that the column was moving at that time away from the theatre of dance and happenings toward the theatre of my life as a personal solution to among other things the Cagian philosophy—which I had until then taken seriously in the context of other people's work—of the continuity and inseparability of life and art. Gradually the life became the theatre became the column. The life being everything of course included everything. Sex was especially interesting since I was in love with a beautiful girl and we were having a very good time of it, at home and on the road. This was embarrassing. I didn't really want to make trouble for myself. Nobody ever gave me reason to believe that I would be adored and acclaimed for loving my own sex.

I was legally married once and for that good behavior I received lots of encouragement and congratulations. Not too much from the spouse himself. Whenever he was greatly angry he would imply that I was homosexual. He was right but I was also heterosexual and living out the part of my karma that had to be with a man and exercise the female function in reproduction. I wasn't thinking. Who thinks. Nor do I think now that I should have been thinking. One think is certain: I was sexually confused and didn't know who I was. My heterosexuality was a flash in the pan you might say. And bisexuality in feeling or practice is too precarious for most people in our society strictured by the absolute heterosexual structuring based on the family unit which drives the homosexual underground. The structure of the society doesn't correspond to our bisexual needs, I don't want to argue bisexuality. In my best moments, I feel trans-sexual and relate to the classical and ancient myths of the sacred character of the androgynous creature, which is rooted in our primordial biological origins. As a mortal A.D. 1970 American I believe that the early family dynamic of each individual creates a predilection for one sex or the other accompanied by a powerful cultural prejudice which favors the choice by each sex of its opposite number. It is the conflict between the culture and the *feelings* of the individual whose objects are made extremely unavailable which constitutes "the homosexual problem." As a latent heterosexual I received the greatest encouragement to express the latent, or least inclined, aspect of myself. Typically, having fulfilled the reproductive function, I was ready to match my object with my deepest feelings but the objects were much less available than a couple of pre-marriage innocent homosexual relationships had led me to believe. I can only imagine that in very favorable conditions the least inclined aspect of one's sexuality might flourish in accord with the social demand. The odds make it unlikely. The course of action then becomes hazardous. The double life of the homosexual is not a sickness he would wish for himself. The bizarre styles of a type of homosexual who has "come out" in the past, besides facilitating identification one by the other, are the witty and angry parodies conforming, by confronting, the stereotyped ideas of a confused public. The latent heterosexual whose true homosexual feelings survive the cultural prejudice is in the outcast unviable position which the current gay activist movements are dedicated to making apparent. I stress that our sexuality is defined by our feelings. Freud on Leonardo: "For it is not the actual activity, but the nature of the feeling which decides for us whether we should attribute to anyone the characteristic of homosexuality." The homosexual whose feelings have been thwarted, repressed by the demands of a heterosexual society, is a confused person, out of touch with his feelings and very often acting in contradiction to his real needs. The gay movement is stressing the positive identity of the homosexual. The key phrase is COME OUT. Come out of hiding. Identify yourself: Make it clear. Celebrate your sexuality

Notwithstanding the hostility of heterosexual men to the homosexual woman, I can say that since my personal campaign to "come out" I have never liked men better and wish they would like me as well. And I hope the heterosexual women also get it together. Just yesterday a heterosexual (-ly inclined) female friend told me she was afraid to be seen with me for what people would say. I thanked her for saying it and went on to scream about the total situation and felt paranoid and angry and revolutionary. The men intimidate the women (a man actually had told her that I was trying to make her homosexual) and divide the women against the women in their fear of losing their objects. To a lesser degree the women keep their men in tow by similar intimidations. It's so confusing I want to drop it. In the spirit of the day my friend Ann says she wants a homosexual experience and I'm doing another weird number by insisting on her heterosexuality (all agreed upon) probably so I can have one heterosexual female friend left who loves me no matter what. I wouldn't speak to her when she turned up at a gay women's dance, and on the way to the Gay-In at Sheep's Meadow I said so I suppose you think you might pass for homosexual. There is some irony but purpose in an over-reactive allegiance to a new found confirmed sexuality, parallel to the kind of reverse prejudice being shown by the new beautiful blacks toward the whites whose color they once thought to be desirable. Also an exaggerated stance is a way of repressing the latent feelings which once confused the issue by receiving cultural encouragement obscuring the deeper need. And an exaggerated stance can clarify one's availability to whom. I want friendships with men that are purged of the availability confusion. Other problems are created in relating to women whose latent homosexuality was never expressed who may be conscious or not and who can make a lot of trouble when the consciousness is low. The issue all the way around is mutual respect.

Jesse Falstein of the Gay Liberation Front says "once we take the risk of admitting that we're beautiful perhaps we have the strength to make the world believe it."

Ann says that as a homosexual and a woman and an artist I'm in a hopeless position. There is nothing to do then but to take it all on. I indicated above that I began declaring my sexuality in the column here in the context of the illustration of my life as total theatre. Truth to the life as a theatre. That's right. But I must add now that already by then (a year and a half ago) I was personally militant about my homosexuality. I had been misbehaving at the heterosexual loft artist parties for instance. Dancing with my heterosexual female friends, if they would. Things like that. Angry. I was angry. I saw nothing in the society around me to affirm a sexual choice that finally I had to make to clarify my life. Nothing except a possible stray lost girl looking for a temporary mother which I wasn't (two children notwithstanding). I never made the underworld gay bar scene. Didn't want to. I was a stray lost girl myself. I didn't know what to do. And I found out that two stray lost girls together make up a frightened team.

It was all far from clear. Anyway it was a stray lost girl team that I made in '64–'65 terminating in the beautiful disaster of Bellevue which caused me to conceive the wildest schemes for personal happiness. I would destroy the psychiatric profession, for a start. I would cause an international scandal by publicly seducing Queen Elizabeth and Jackie Kennedy and Liz Taylor and such like media dishes. I would save the world which desperately needed to be saved from its wickedness in depriving me of my personal happiness. I hatched a plan a minute. And did nothing. Except to tell my friends, who already knew, that I was homosexual. But I was on the way and didn't know it. The more I said it the more familiar it sounded. The more familiar it sounded the more I began to think I really was what I said I was. The more certain I was of what I said I was the more I began to be what I was according to what I said I was in short and long, I did something about it. The more I said it and was it and did it the more confident and integrated I began to feel frankly like a person instead of a stray lost girl waiting once a decade for another stray lost girl to happen to fall into bed after a drunken heterosexual party. I was a hopeless case as it were. So by accident I gave birth to myself. One day in 1965 I lay down on a bed and had enormous labor pains for as long as it took to give birth to myself. Subsequently I went to sleep for a long time. Then I woke up and recalled my second birth. Then I went to sleep again and gradually reawakened to my new self which had some new ways of writing and dressing and talking and thinking—mostly being.

Last week at a GLF meeting as part of the gay celebration week Sidney Abbot said "lesbian women are the ones who early perceived the oppression of women." I don't know. I don't think I early perceived much of anything. There certainly wasn't a white suprematist male chauvinist capitalist pig around. Wrong. I had a white suprematist male chauvinist pig called Eddie, a second cousin who came over once a week to give me a piano lesson and eat a piece of pie and play a game of pick-up-sticks. He was very good humoured and lived quite happily with his aging mother. No, for me it's a downner and a bummer to dwell on the oppression of women. I see that women are oppressed. I hope for the alleviation of all oppression. (The movement has raised my consciousness, i.e., at a dinner in L.A. with one heterosexual girl and three heterosexual men I said I wasn't going to listen to a whole evening of male accomplishments; I heard the set in the opening remarks.) But oppression is a worldwide interfamilial interstate intercontinental interpersonal phenomenon. It is a prime fact of a political structure. I can't dwell on our oppression and remain a relatively liberate fugitive artist. Oppression is real. Our lives are illusory. Men and women are real. Our sexual differentiation is illusory. Space and time are real. There is no past present or future. We are living in the past the present and the future which is an eternal present. We appear to be becoming but in reality we are being in the everlasting now. If the now is not a beautiful present when will we be beautiful? The talk of oppression is about a beautiful future. An oppressed person becomes beautiful in the presence of a beautiful presence. At the meetings I have felt an absence of spirituality and cosmic consciousness. In San Francisco at the Family Dog Auditorium once a week a few thousand far out longhairs gather to unite in being and to gather strength to go out to infect the world with being. At the Gay-In in Sheep's Meadow the oppressed homosexuals united for an afternoon of expressing being. In celebrating my being I can't accept any program for resisting or attacking "the enemy" such as feminist Ti-Grace Atkinson advocates in the struggle for liberation of women. Ti-Grace spoke at the Daughters of Bilitis during the gay week. She says that men are the enemy and she speaks of spikes and armor and militant tactics and ideological pitfalls and the murders of feminist revolutionaries in Russia in 1919 and the vaginal orgasm as a mass hysterical survival response and frightening things like that. I like Ti-Grace and I'd like to help her by going to bed with her but I think she needs intensive bio-energetic Reichian therapy by a male chauvinist pig who wouldn't rape her or redeem her but who would be kind to her. I wasn't too kind at her lecture when I called out a proposition for bed. I only half meant it, I was putting her on—she defines feminism as a theory and lesbianism as a practice—and challenging her address to lesbian women who feel like the arch feminists. I meant the proposition in part as a gesture of affirmation of the body which looks to me on her to be disconnected from her head which thinks a great deal in the university tradition. Denying her body to men as a political tactic seems a maneuver consistent with her radical feminist position; but a body I assume to be bound up in its armor of fear and hatred of an "enemy" who never satisfied it will project and sublimate the frustration into a political rationale that sounds hysterical to me. I don't think Ti-Grace is inclined toward her own sex (either). She's a brave girl. She told the audience at some point that we had had an "encounter"—which we did last January. I've known her for a few years but formerly within the art world. I saw her at a party in a Peck and Peck type outfit that I didn't believe and I knew what she was into so I made a move as a gesture instinctively toward something I wasn't sure what. At the lecture last week she posed some interesting questions. First off she countered my challenge by defining and denouncing it as behavior belonging to the male psychology. I'm glad she said that. It illustrates our stereotyped ideas of role-playing passivity and aggression. Arlene Kisner of the GLF said that any time a woman asserts her own desires and needs does not mean she is showing male psychology. I'm not excusing myself. There was a fair bit of hostility in the scene I made. My program for self identity sometimes includes aggressive posturing that belies a sexually passive nature. But I don't think Ti-Grace had mere aggression in mind. Part of her feminist rationale is that the female dynamic is love and the male dynamic is sex. Translated Man-Sex-Evil. Versus: Woman-Love-Good. Further translation: superiority of mind and spirit in the Puritan box of horrors derived from every Christian medieval dualistic dogma for salvation and damnation. I tell you it blows my head out. We want to get things together and there's always the old kind of divisiveness in a new disguise. Ti-Grace also brought up the subject of whore houses which we discussed, or I belabored, a few month ago. She says there must be something wrong if ... in the tradition of a crusading zeal for reforming prostitution. Eliminating would be the word I guess. I wanted to make it clear it isn't the whore house in actuality that interests me as a possibility for women, necessarily. It's the whore house as an arch symbol of the man's more extensive recognized sexuality. Why are there no zoos or baths or houses for women? In L.A. a haterosexual man said to me but women don't need whore houses, they can have a man any time they want. Maybe so, but they can't *pay* for the *specific* satisfactions they might want that are not available in a prosaic married or unmarried life. I don't believe anything is wrong anywhere. Whatever, it seems to me the idea is to expand our sexual potential to meet the greater freedom of the male for variety and quantity, so forth. Ann has a house rap that goes like how to begin with all the rooms have holes so she can watch everybody, especially a rape scene; a room with people in costumes with their genitals exposed; a room with cupids and roses and velvet swings; and a room with sinks with men doing the dishes being sucked off by 11 year old girls. Sometimes we have sex for tricks and sometimes for feeling, sometimes a feeling turns into a trick or a trick a feeling or a tricky feeling and when it all comes together it's fabulous, isn't it? Woe and behold! Someday I'll give it all up to contemplate my navel.

Coda for the celebration of the new gay: Read Colette's "The Pure and the Impure"—: "A woman finds pleasure in caressing a body whose secrets she knows, her own body giving her the clue to its preferences ... And the shadow projected on the intervening space need not be that worst intruder, a man. The most ordinary irruption can mortally change the steady hothouse warmth in which two women devote themselves to the cultivation of a delusion." "In May 1778, two wellborn young girls, related to the Welsh aristocracy, ran away together and, having chosen their fate, cloistered their solitude, their reciprocal tenderness for 53 years, in Llangollen, a small town in Wales. Lady Eleanor Butler, the elder of the two, died at the age of 90 ... At the source of their serenity, going back a half century, they at least could find, still warm in its ashes, the romantic memory of their first elopement, the wild race at night on foot through mountainous roads, their feet bleeding in fragile cloth slippers ... they could remember two nights out in the open, sleeping in a ruined barn, Sarah shivering with cold in spite of the protective arms around her ... nights of anxiety, of mounting fever, and then the approach of pursuers guided by the barking of Sarah's little dog ... infatuated with romance they had leaped from a window rather than leave by way of the open door ... they corresponded with each other by secret means, bribed servants, and at the moment of leaving, had seized firearms they did not know how to use and fled on horseback, although they had never in their lives sat a horse ... there were complications, legal processes, tragedies, childish tears ... but from all this a unique sentiment sprang, straight and firm and flowering like the iris nestling against its green stem ... What did they want? Almost nothing. Everything. They wanted to live together. When at last the two families yielded, overwhelmed, unable to make head or tail of this folly, of this pure but irregular passion, the two girls suddenly became as gentle as tame doves ... the matter was settled. A vow of reclusion descended on this couple of young girls, separating them from the world, veiling and changing and remaking the universe in their eyes ... We would know nothing more of the Ladies of Llangollen, had not the elder according to the fashion of the time kept a diary only twice interrupted in 13 years. The younger, Sarah, was called Beloved and Better Half and Delight of my Heart."

From the diary: "A day of the most perfect and sweet retirement."

"Rose at seven. A sweet spring morning. Ten. My beloved and I drank a dish of tea. A day of the most delicious and exquisite retirement."

"Writing, drawing, sweet sunshine, blue sky. Soft smoke from the village ascending in spirals. Birds innumerable."

"Soft fine rain. My Beloved and I went the Home Circuit. Celestial lovely day."

"My Beloved and I gathered holly berries, primrose and strawberry plants for our Banks ... then visited a cow, saw her suckling her son, went to the new garden, gathered gooseberries. The country in a blaze of beauty."

BASH IN THE SCULLS

1970-08-13

EAST HAMPTON—One acre of love sun and sound at the Sculls. Drive along a Georgica road where the rich inherited the earth of East Hampton. An open sesame table at the head of the gravel driveway. Smiling women for equality. They say well look at list five other people called in to come for the Voice. Barbara Guest parries all checkshuns and leads me dancing and singing by the hand down the yellow brick road to the Crossbones. No she didn't but she was just charming and also flatterfull of good will too. This party I think Tom Wolfe would identifry it as Radical Chick for Women Striking for Equality later on this month after reseiving the necessary funds from such parties as these that Bob an Ethel Scull sponsored at 25 grubs a poison to see their premises. That's not true but it's the way Bob himself now striding tord me cross his greeny lawn in his ducky white pants and candy striped shirt open at a mossy chest and his new Commander Whitehead beard under a rich smile did put it that people would be paying to see the place. He's happy to see me and so am I. Nice little bungalow you've got her Bob. Mmmm. I can't give you the style number and we're not allowed in, it's a lawn party, but it's a right angulated one story black and white and windowy modern minimal everybody's building/ Some are building monuments/ Others are jotting down notes. All my colleagues in the crime of reporting I never meant. Charlotte Curtis. Time. Newsday. Swiss Television. United Press. International Syndicated News Service. Once

I mingled in a group of five of which four of us were taking notes. My editor (there too perchance) said it's the ultimate sort of party where nobody shows up except the people who write about it. I tried interviewing Charlotte Curtis who was interviewing two men who might've been interviewing her while a lady was interrupting to interview me about whatever went wrong between Betty Friedan and me. What went wrong between Betty Friedan and me was a lapse of sexual interest. I liked her below the chin and was ready to talk at that level but she got super huffy when I arsked if there shouldn't be a pub(l)ic conjunction between Women's Liberation and the Gay Liberation Front. Her eyes went big 'n bulgy and her lipstick leered crimson and she said crisply enunciating each word that "it" is not an issue. What? She repeated. *And*, there's no relationship between the movements. Well, and she softened a moment. I am against all oppression. Good, but don't you think...—and she waved me off, excuse me I have other important things to do as she spun on her maxi and I called out after her you mean "it" is embarrassing. And Scull standing there looking at his feet his hands folded at the duck white pants behind over the coccyx. He wanders me a tour of the lawn garden fountain sculpture layout. Here's a tomato red tube fabricated Alexander Lieberman. It matches your napkin Bob. Mmmm. A stainless steel Walter de Maria cage. A neon number. A gray minimal Morris he called a do-nut, it has a square hole. A wood beam di Suvero faded weathering beautifully into driftwood. A fountain of three di Suvero cast bronze hands, and the story to go with it about how the one hand where the water sprouts out of its palm was supposed to cost 400 and Mark demanded 4 thou and got it and Scull says to me you know that Mark insults me, calls me a robber baron and the worst names—and I love him. He's beaming. Unhhuh, ... you've changed Bob. *Yeah*, I feel *great*, just great. He looks yachtsman cocktails. Tanned and supersuccessful. His wife Ethel is standing near the mikes by the pool in a quilted maxi looking slim and Betsy Ross-ish. He turns and smiles and says fondly you know we've been married 26 years. By the pool. The pool! Don't Go Near the Water! The pool is the centerpieces here the perfect aqua rectangle undisturbed by its peripheral human slow motion of cameras cocktails interviews. Back in the bushes by a road bordering the lawn sits a barefoot guerrilla. Why donchu come in I called out. Because I don't have $25. I was near him and I turned and scanned my sister and fellow guests and when I saw the host of the Philistines I was afraid and my heart greatly trembled. No it didn't. But *lo* a voice from heaven, saying, This is my beloved Daughter in whom I am (not) so well pleased. It was time. Something had to happen here. A new historical folks pass. In a flash I turned into a One Eyed One Horned Flying Purple People Eater. No I didn't. I continued interviewing and being interviewed. I talk to Edith de Rham who wrote *her* book one year after (in '64) Betty Friedan did and who saw that women didn't have the freedom she had in being able to pay for a maid. I say then you must've had an experience that wasn't so pleasant to make you that sympathetic. Yes, she was married before her present marriage and with*out* the money for a maid and she wanted to jump off a bridge from it. Right. It had eluded me that the movement had so much to do with maids. We need a better distribution of maids. Maids for everybody. Maids for the MAIDS. I decide to test her on the gay issue which Betty Friedan said is not an issue. She isn't hysterical like Betty but torrentially defensive. You see we don't hate men and so forth. And a story about a "queer" designer who was always describing his fabulous mother. I register that she's had gay men figured out for some time. Mother will never be duplicated. I change the subject and suggest that the women who hate men the most (and vice versa) are those who go to bed with them. She doesn't like any of it anyway and gives the old one-two about being normal or natural in preferring her opposite. "I'm not narcissistic you see." St John of the Cross where are you:/ There is in every perfect love/ A law to be accomplished too:/ That the lover should resemble/ The belov'd: and be the same/ And the greater is the likeness/ Brighter will the rapture flame—Narcissime: qui consiste a se choisir soi-meme come object erotique.—Our interview was being interrupted by another.

Edith's book by the way was "The Love Fraud" and I'm sorry I don't know what it's about a fraud I guess. She said she's happily married now. Who can I seduce here. Betty wears lipstick. Ethel is busy being hostess. Barbara disappeared. Charlotte is taking notes. My editor is here with her boyfriend. So I'm talking to Scull again over a manicured hedge. Admiring his Commander Whitehead beard, just the right dash of distinguished gray-white in a black brush as clipped as the hedge is. Schwebbers Electronics has that kind of beard now too. Scull is expansive suddenly: I can't *wait* to see my depressions in Nevada. Your *What*?—My depressions.—Oh. My sculpture in the desert in Nevada, by Mike Heizer. Oh. Say Bob who's that? I've spied my quarry across the pool. Pale blue cycle shades. That's Gloria Steinem. Gloria! Terrific. I made haste round the pool through the cameras cocktails interviews. She's in a bare-back and just as pretty at eyeball distance. Our past and future is settled immediately. Midwest-Smith-India-New York Magazine. And I disclose my unscheduled pool event. Return in peace to the ocean, my love; I too am part of that ocean, ... we are not so much separated ...—We are instantly by an introduction from Betty Friedan who's been giving a pep talk at the mikes about Women for Equality. She introduces Gloria. I wander back the other side of the pool, the hedge side. I was coming into that abnormal condition known as elation. I would cast my swine before pearls and give that which is unholy to the daubs. I would return my body to the water (Gene before he died said he was returning the earth to the land as he threw his flower pots from fifth story to sidewalk). And I lectured my brethren: the proper posture is to listen and to learn from lunatics as in former times. No I didn't. I sat down to organize the explosion. Removal of pants shoes socks hardware. I had to leave my notes behind. Too bad. I walk quickly to the center of the shallow end. Almost fall skidding on the slippery edge. Last Chance Balloon. Tarzana from the trees at cocktails. I didn't cross myself. I didn't yell geronimo. I dove in and did my lengths. I hoped my colleague reporters would be noting my 10 point Australian crawl. I did a little exhibition breast stroke as well. The second time round I got rid of the faded blue railroad shirt with a hole in the sleeve (Yes it was a calculated costume). She's terrible, she's beautiful. She isn't beautiful, she isn't terrible enough. Anyway I was alone in the aquarium. Water lovely. No rubber ducky (in the tubby). I emerge. Slippery edge. Jill tombe pour la seconde fois. Scull is waiting eagerly with big yellow towel and so happily I think he's my trainer and I just won the race. I go beyond the hedge into the trees. A maxi lady is lurking in the bushes WHY DID YOU DO THAT? I mean but extremely furious. I'm wiping the chlorine out of my eyes. It isn't self-evident. Well ... I was ... uh ... hot—and drunk. HOT. And DRUNK.—God, where's my notebook. The other notebooks are coming tord me fast now. They're saying you were hot and drunk. *Were* you hot and drunk? Yes. Were you protesting? Yes. Are you a woman ...? Yes. Were you part of a Red Stocking Plot to Sabotage this Party? Yes. Were you showing off? Yes. Are you a radical lesbian? Yes. Do you like the Sculls? Sure. Did Mr. Scull put you up to it? No. He neither endorsed nor discouraged the exhibition but I did get permission from my editor. *WHY* did you do it? Well ... I think one should be serious in one's purposes but not necessarily solemn. Well ... Have gun, will travel. See pool, will swim. Well ... It was a Conceptual Swim. Well you see I have this reportsibility to make my life interesting to my readers each week. And then I stormed the mikes and lectured my brethren again: Except ye become as little children ye can in no vice exit the killdom of haven. No I didn't. I went behind a tree to write up my swim. Scull appeared. They're saying I put you up to it. Well just say I was hot and drunk. And offer me a dry shirt please. He gets another blue workshirt. Where's Gloria? They're not even thanking me for the awful time I gave them. No, it's getting all changed around. You were great. Terrific. Sensational. Verweile doch, du bist so schon. But Gloria won't dance. Betty is still put out. Ethel and Edith and Charlotte disappeared along with Barbara. A voice on the mikes is saying Ladies and gentlemen the party is over. Radical Chick is over. One acre of love sun and sound. Was there any perfecting of spirits here this afternoon? I'd like to leave my clothes impaled on a souvenir spear. Tell it all, brother and sisters. Dinner at the Silver Sea Horse. The Wheel of Wandering On.

ON A CLEAR DAY YOU CAN SEE YOUR MOTHER

1971-05-06

Some old lines and some new ones thrown on to each other for the Town Hall affair

The title of this episode is new approach: All women are lesbians except those who don't know it naturally they are but don't know it yet I am a woman who is a lesbian because I am a woman and a woman who loves herself naturally who is other women is a lesbian a woman who loves women loves herself naturally this is the case that a woman is herself is all woman is a natural born lesbian so we don't mind using the name like any name it is quite meaningless it means naturely I am a woman and whatever I am we are we affirm being what we are the way of course all men are homosexuals being having a more sense of their homo their homo-ness their ecce homoness their ecce prince & lord & master-ness the 350 years of Abraham intersample Abraham lived for 350 years because the bible ages are only a succession of sons and fathers and grandfathers intensely identifying with their ancestors their son so identified naturely with the father that he believed he was the father and of course he was as was Abraham and Isaac and Jacob and Esau and Reuben and Simeon and Levi and Judah and Joseph each one lived for 350 years, but who are the daughters of Rachel and Ruth and

Sarah and Rebekah the rest we do not know the daughters never had any daughters they had only sons who begat more sons and sons so we have very little sense, from that particular book, of the lineage and ligaments and legacies and identities of mothers and daughters and their daughters and their mothers and mothers and daughters and sisters who were naturally not lesbians if they had nothing of each other save sons so now we must say Verily Verily, I say unto thee, except a woman be born again she cannot see the Kingdom of Goddess a woman must be born again to be herself her own eminence and grace the queen queen-self whose mother has pressed upon her mouth innumerable passionate kisses so sigh us … There is in every perfect love/ A law to be accomplished too: that the lover should resemble/ The belov'd: And be the same. And the greater is the likeness/ Brighter will the rapture flame—even as John there St. John of the Cross raptured on his pal Jesus whose son he was his father his son as when Jesus in another time said to his lovers and haven't you heard it a deluge of times And he saith unto them, Follow me, and I will make you fishers of men. And straightway they left their nets, and followed him. Ah lover and perfect equal! I meant that you should discover me so, by my faint indirection; And I, when I meet you, mean to discover you by the like in you … I want she who is the tomboy in me … I want she who is very female in me … I want she who is British about me … I want she who is ugly American about me … I want she who is mayonnaise about me … I want she who is the cunt and the balls and the breasts of me and the long straight browny hair and the gangly boarding school adolescent in a navy blue blazer and gold buttons of me … narcissme, qui consiste a se choisir soimeme comme objet erotique … and I want the men to carry my boxes of books for me and carry me upsy daily pigback and pay for me everywhere and adore me as a lesberated woman Over the inevitable we shall not grieve … This is the body that Jill built … Ecce Leda the Lesbian … Ecce Greta the Gay the gay Gertrude the gay gay gayness of being gay, of being, to be equal we have to become who we really are and women we will never be equal women until we love one another women and say Woe, and behold, a voice from Hera saying This is my beloved daughter in whom I am well pleased O Women of America the World you are your own best friend, your own closest friend, you are the best company for yourself ... you should go through and study even right back to your childhood, and of course if you have the great ability to go back to your previous lives you should do so Women of America the World you are your own best friend ... These are the series of sayings we are saving the world with: the lamentations of Mary and Marilyn Monroe. Lord help you, Maria, full of grease, the load is with me! Her smile is between her legs and her moustache is in her armpit and she ordered that history should begin with her with her this is a muster of elephental cuntsequence the lost and foundamental situation of the feminine is the primordial relation of identity between mother and daughter the mysteries of Eleusis of the reunion of Demeter and her daughter Persephone to be born again and again and Arethusa and Artemis and Hebe and Hera and Diana and Daphne and Doris and Dora and Dolly and the Danaides all but one murdered their husbands on their wedding nights our case revives their stories for more than a hundred years I wander about in it without coming to the end of her body the most we can do is to dream the myth onwards, and rewrite the stories we will reunite Electra and her mother Clytemnestra and Jocasta will be well pleased in her daughter Antigone who will be more involved in her mothers and her daughters than in the proper burial for her brother and we will remember the histories of say how Eleanor of Aquitaine made a crusade to the holy land and dressed all her ladies in waiting as Amazons in leopard skins and dressed herself as Pan Athenea and that's how they rode through Greece for the queendom of heaven is as a woman travelling into a far country who called her own servants and delivered unto them *her* goods for Whole the World to see a woman finds pleasure in caressing a body whose secrets she knows, her own body giving her the clue to its preferences giving each the other their sense of self tracing the body of the woman whose fingers in turn trace her body that the miracle of the mirror be accomplished between women love is contemplative caresses are intended less to gain possession of the other than gradually to recreate the self thru her own self among the women and the women the multitude on the way to the way the world was before it began it is now the world is heading definitely towards a matriarchy more often to return to the source of things we must travel in the opposite direction, Wring out the clothes! Wring in the dew! Before all the King's Hoarsers with all the Queens Mum Her birth is uncontrollable and her organ is working perfectly and there's apart that's not screwed on and her education is now for by and about women and presided over by woman All women are lesbians except those who don't know it of course since whereas both sexes (even as Sigmund sd) are originally more attached to the mother and it is the *task* of the girl to transfer this attachment to the father naturally they we are but don't know it yet that woman is now approaching her ancient destiny as woman I am and therefore lesbian which means nothing we could say it over and over again over lesbianlesbianlesbianlesbianlesbianlesbianlesbian lesbian—Special from the White House, the President of the United States announced last night the appointment of a lesbian to his cabinet ... it's nice if you can invite them in, they usually come in without knocking ... Womens lib and let lib new official position on lesbians: Hey ladies it's okay, like Red China is there so we might as well recognize it ... yupyop ... Liberal Schmiberal ... Maybe ... uh ... we should invite ... uh ... her ... uh ... one of them to dinner ... One of what, dear? Uh, well, uh, she is a bit odd isn't she? I mean, you know how we'd feel if a black man was interested in our daughter—Aaaaaaaaaaaa ... Oh god, and she might make a pass at my wife ... Agh ... But if she just doesn't *talk* about what she is ... We could pretend ... Whaddyou say to the naked lady please please sorry thank you we are getting to the bottom of women's lib we are going down on women's lib I am beside myself with love for you when you are beside me my love the beginning of the unifirst is rite now if all tinks are at this momentum being cremated and the end of the unihearse is right now for all thinks are at this momentus passing away we went to see the Dairy of a Skinzopretty girl O why dint her mother straighten out her teeth when she was young O she is envolved in many strange and wondrous adventures O in short she had come into that abnormal condition known as elation O she did not yet love and she loved to love; she sought what she might love, in love with loving ... O what can she say now that is not the story of so many others O do not fail me she says you are my last chance, indeed our last chance, to save the West ... and who vants the Moon ven ve can land on Venus ... and O how would you like to be the heroine of yr own life story (she's looking forward to it extremely) and O don't be nervous be mermaid be she whom I love who travels with me and sits along while holding me by the hand she ahold of my hand has completely satisfied me o natural woman woman vimmin virmin woreman woeman of America the World until until women all the women see in each other the possibility of a primal commitment which includes sexual love they will be denying themselves the love and value they have readily accorded to men, thus affirming their second class status for within the heterosexual institution no woman can be the equal it is a contrafiction in terms the heterosexual institution is a male institution a homo ecce homo institution and you can't ever change the absoluteness the institution is political is built out of the institutionalized slavery of women so it is a contradiction in terms—such an institution must only collapse of its own accord from within the heterosexual institution is over spiritually over and the new thing now that is happening is the withdrawal of women to give each other their own sense of self a new sense of self until women see in each other the possibility of a primal commitment which includes sexual love they will be denying themselves the love and value they readily accord to men thus affirming their second class status. *Until all women are lesbians there will be no true political revolution* until in other same words we are woman I am a woman who loves herself naturally who is other women is a lesbian a woman who loves women loves herself naturally this is the case that a woman is herself is all woman is a natural born lesbian so we don't mind using the name it means naturely I am a woman and whatever I am we are we affirm being what we are saying therefore *Until all women are lesbians there will be no true political revolution* meaning the terminus of the heterosexual institution through the recollection by woman of her womanhood her own grace and eminence by the intense identities of our ancestors our descendants of the mothers and the daughters and the grandmothers we become who we are which is to say we become our own identities and autonomies even as now we are so but except those who don't know it yet will be quite upset about it for some time to come as I would more properly be as majorities would have it leaning on my sword describing my defeat some women want to have their cock and eat it too and lesbian is a label invented by anybody to throw at any woman who dares to be a man's equal and lesbian is a good name it means nothig of course or everythig so we don't mind using the name in face we like it for we can be proud to claim allusion to the island made famous by Sappho the birds are talking to us in Greek again and continue on making a big thing out of it over all these centuries time we can do that we don't mind it's nice in fact for we all all of us women are lesbians why not and isn't it wonderful what a lot of devotion there is to us lying around the universe especially to those all envolved in some penis they're wrapping their cunts around ... Oh well ... Lillian over and out ... he sd I want your body and she sd you can have it when I'm through with it ... Keep yer hands off me you worldwide weirdo, I just want to be noticed, not attacked—we had a big argonaut about it ... The age of shrivelry is abonus again ... A Lord was not considered defeated in a local war until his flag had fallen from the main tower of his castle ... svastickles falling outen da sky ... the current dispute would be settled if the central figure was no longer present *(at this moment our leader Norman Mailer akst me to read my last line and I said I'd like to forego the question and my friends appeared on stage and I made love before notables and my circuitry got overloaded and the men in the audience voted they dint want to hear me no more and I don't remember too much except leaving and wishing later I'd kissed Germaine before we walked off)* ... Flash from the White House: last night the President of the

United States, clad only in a scanty tribal costume, announced the resignation of the American Government … His life was an empty record of gambling cockfighting titting balls and masques vimmin and vine clothes … Better latent than never … aliquem alium interum … there's no such thing as sexual differentiation in the spiritual nature of wo(man) … This is the problem passion play of the millentury … = this Restoration Comedy—it's going to be a beautiful reunion … plunderpussy and all spoiled goods going into her nabsack and some heroine women in wings of Samothrace … Is it to drown her passengers that you have bored a hole in her? Rubbish, what bunkum these people talk … Events are preshipitaking themselves in the harpiest confusion … cunnilinguist … Listen. If you recognized an aspect of yourself that you love in these ancient new womens heads I too have recognized an admirable aspect of myself in your willingness to be as beautiful as you are who you are My mother was a vestal, my father I knew not no prince nor lord nor master-ness but the nipples and navels of a whirld a wonderwoman the mothers and the daughters and the great grandmothers and daughters of Rachel and Ruth and Sarah and Rebekah the rest we will know now the daughter the mothers and sisters will have daughters who beget daughters so we will more sense, from this time, of the lineage and ligaments and legacies and identities of our mothers and daughters and their mothers and mothers and daughters and sisters who are naturally of course lesbians if they have of each other and saying Verily Verily except a woman must be born again she cannot see the Queendom of goddess a woman must be born again to be herself her own eminence and grace the queen queenself whose mother has pressed upon her mouth innumerable passionate kisses … Sail away where the wind blows sweet … and take a sister by her hand … Lead her far from this barren land … ON A CLEAR DAY YOU CAN SEE YOUR MOTHER.

THE MAKING OF A LESBIAN CHAUVINIST

1971-06-17

Lesbians who are not chauvinists are monogamous. The new liberation front is the lesbian chauvinist movement. A lesbian chauvinist is a woman who enjoys a variety of affectionate and sexual experiences with different members of her own sex. If she marries another woman she no longer qualifies as a chauvinist. Gregory Battcock is the only pure male homosexual chauvinist I know. He says he doesn't try to mess up his boyfriends' minds with love, security, false promises, fidelity, and the like. I asked him what does he do if a lover develops more interest in his person than his attitudes can tolerate. He says then he makes himself as obnoxious as possible, even developing bad breath if necessary. Revolutions are all about language, inventing and distorting your terms to suit the new strategies of survival. Male chauvinism is now a dead phrase. The new lesbian is co-opting it to define her positive attitudes of polygamous independence united with an exclusive interest in her own sex. Such an absurd but real position might more accurately be described by the term chauvinism than the attitudes of the heterosexual male who won the term in its pejorative sense in our time through its revival by the feminists in their proper instinct for a word just obscure enough to express an educated disdain for the cause of their social and private distress. I stopped using the word when I heard the musical "machismo" on the Coast. Now I'm bored with machismo too. I'm bored, in fact, with the problem or the concept. I'm very interested in this new idea of lesbian chauvinism. Derived from Nicolas Chauvin, a soldier of the First Republic and Empire, whose demonstrative patriotism and attachment to Napoleon came to be ridiculed by his comrades, the word has as much relevance to the polygamous lesbian as it did to the American male of choice in the ongoing battleground of language. I wish I had thought it up myself. I'll be satisfied if 1 demonstrate its usefulness to define a situation already long in existence but not socially comprehensible until truly invented by the whimsical dislocation of language to express reversal of value attending the same phrase. It isn't easy to be a lesbian chauvinist. Lots of people still think you're as wicked as the male of that description who owns and runs the world through the elaboration of his sexual preference into the various patterns of subjugation and captivity much noted by the polemical feminists who have realized at last the intimate connection between power, economy, property, and sex. I don't own or run anything except a deteriorating '66 VW van. The most difficult aspect, however, of being a lesbian chauvinist is the problem of maintaining the life style appropriate to our new definition by warding off the temptations of monogamy in a society in which the prime unit of its functioning as a warring nation is its embattled family. Next week I'll redefine my position as a lesbian monogamist. This week the revolution is the liberation of the lesbian chauvinist. The grand edifices of theory and speculation are elegant smokescreens for personal tactics of destruction survival and renewal. I've been a happy chauvinist in spirit since the summer of '68. A lapse or two since then into the exquisite agonies of feudalism or monogamy is not an aspect of my journey I go around boasting about. Not that it matters to anybody. People are learning to ignore the exaggerated claims and denials of their friends and various exhibitionists. People are learning to despise all problems and solutions that aren't their own. People are learning to be severely disappointed by the slightest deviation from any problem or solution that sounded good the week before. As people myself I feel the same way naturally. All we want to do is to dictate our own thrilling letters. All I'd like to do actually is write the feminist version of "My Secret Life." I've been postponing an account of my amorous adventures in London '68 because they seem, at this date, embarrassingly harmless and meagre, and/or because I needed the revolutionary context of the new lesbian chauvinism to make the experiences pertinent to current or ancient issues. In connection with Lois Lane I mentioned that my momentous visit prompted my return to America as "a roaring lesbian." I meant that I discovered I could sleep with a woman and not feel like it was the beginning or the end of the world. Meaning that it was possible to just go to bed and have a good time and get up and share a cup of coffee or not even do that and say goodbye and thank you quite amicably like any self respecting male chauvinist for whom the pleasures of the body are not necessarily complicated and constrained by the emotions of greed envy fear guilt anger jealousy etcetera all the defensive-aggressive equipment attending the onset of romantic love. The British taught me this lesson. They were very hard on me. I arrived a gaping tourist and left a hardened sexist. Not really, I cried all the way home. I don't remember why. But I remained as mushy as I ever was which was pretty mushy. Possibly I hadn't grasped yet that it wasn't a crime to fall in love with every British princess who seemed as interested as I was in the mere pleasures of the body. Actually, there were only three. I think. That was enough. For a three week visit the average was outstanding. For a pure innocent virginal American it was lurid and licentious. For a victim of lesbian monogamy it was a revelation. Having dutifully tramped through Westminster and St. Paul's and Charing Cross and the National Museum and Trafalgar Square and Picadilly Circus and the subway system and Soho and the Tower and around the Palace & so forth one day I decided impulsively I had to visit a gay bar. I had never done this in my life before. Except once as a very young lesbian naturally not connecting my thinking with my activities, therefore imagining I was a nice normal person, I went slumming with a friend to a Village place, meaning a low down dive, to watch the freaks and get excitedly aghast at *members of the same sex dancing together!* By the summer of '68 if you can believe it I guess you can I was still disconnected in this way my thinking or my attitudes or prejudices and my true nature were distinctly and neurotically separate from each other. I was a walking contradiction in turns. I just couldn't see myself as a freak. It was bad enough I was too tall for my age and wore my freckles when the sun came out. I was even strolling around in those fashionable gabardine culottes or leather mini skir's, I must have looked ridiculous. A lesbian still pretending she was available for invasion. Anyway, I went all out for some inexplicable reason and learned about a place called the Gates or Gateways Club. George Brecht located it for me. Very reluctantly. He said he was disappointed in me. I guess he thought he had an exclusive patent on chauvinism, not that I knew at the time that's what he was. I assumed all men had the right to drink a lot and insult womankind and drag as many as possible off by the hair into their caves. So naturally he was not enthusiastic about being an accomplice to my initiation as a rival chauvinist of the lesbian variety. Not that either of us knew the ultimate significance of his innocent investigation. The Gates, by the way, is the bar that figured as the freak joint in "The Killing of Sister George," which I saw a few months later in New York. The entrance had a speakeasy feeling about it. You'd never see it if you didn't know where it was exactly. The door opened directly on a flight of stairs leading down to I imagined a dark den of sin. It was just a smallish well lit rather cheery basement room with comfortable round booths, a bar, a jukebox. The woman at the bottom of the stairs was a hardened something or other. Dressed high femme lipstick earrings stocking heels etc. with an incongruously low dark voice and garish features. The bartenders were handsome heavy set butch a type that has always repelled bewildered and frightened me. I sat down and waited. Eventually the only other customer addressed me sort of luke over her shoulder from her position turned three quarters away from me. I could appreciate her bleached blond straight short hair and middling cockney accent. Hearing my own American she warmed up and even not too much later turned round to face me. She introduced herself as Maureen. She got so warm in fact she was inviting me to her place to meet her roommate who "likes American girls" and her own lover who was an ex-patriot American. I said I'd like to do that but later on if possible after I found out what this bar was all about. Soon I found out. It seemed the entire gay woman population of London must have decided this was the place to be that night. I had no idea there were so many gay people. I was very embarrassed. I didn't know what to do. I suppose I just sat there transfixed with horrified curiosity. I had a very snobbish attitude. I'm sure I didn't think I was a lesbian too. Yet I was rigged out to conform to one of the two stereotyped roles obtaining in conventional gay society until recently. Excepting my long hair. But they overlooked the hair because of my tie. The tie seemed to guarantee my role as a female who would play the part of a male. In my three lesbian marriages I had never played any part whatsoever unless it was all parts, so I regarded the attitude with amused toleration, thankful to be attractive to one half of the jam-packed room for inadvertently wearing the right thing. A year later I returned sans tie and was so confusing apparently to everybody that I became a model wallflower. Or else I had aged considerably. Or they had caught on to me. Or some damned thing. I didn't seriously figure any of this out until recently. Some experienced friends have by now explained the customs. I don't like any of them. No self respecting lesbian likes them. Aside from the exorbitant mafia prices of drinks or minimum the bars are corroded with long centuries psychologies of self hatred addressed to everybody. And the frantic behaviour of excessive monogamous thinking, quite naturally, since self hatred breeds extremely precarious relationships and the lesbian is not yet liberated into her chauvinism. I learned fast at the Gates. I asked someone the time and was threatened with murder by her girlfriend. I supposed she was desperate. It was a good thing I just asked the time. I realized right then I'd better not make a move to talk or dance or anything or they'd be flying me home as a corpse. So I waited. I didn't wait too long. I was pretty popular as I said. Thus there were a succession of sidewise or bizarre approaches. All femmes. I was a butch! The most exciting proposition was a note pressed into my hand by the femme I thought to be the most beautiful in the place; she was so expert in her treachery, passing the message on the run as it were and no doubt while her "steady" was collecting their coats and momentarily out of sight. It was really dramatic. A sequence in a spy movie. I repaired to the ladies right away to read it and find her name and a telephone no. scrawled in pencil. I took the names and numbers of two others who weren't as spectacular in their looks or approach and left to go to Maureen's flat to see about her roommate who "likes American girls." I felt saturated by London lesbiana. I felt I had learned something. I didn't know what exactly. Probably my unconscious was fast at work transforming me overnight into a raging chauvinist. One thing was certain. It no longer seemed bizarre for two members of the same sex to be dancing together. One other thing was certain. There were lots of lesbians in the world. Maybe half the world were lesbians. And I suppose I left with the faint suspicion that I too might be one of them.

SOCIALS WIT JOG & YOKEL

1971-07-01

Thursday June 24 10 a.m. arise go collect a passport and ticket to Paris and call David Bourdon who already called to leave message that he was not going to do anything about changing the Yoko film times because the woman from Life can't come any earlier or later than 3 and that he was paralyzed and wouldn't call Dan Richter. None of this has to make sense and if it seems funny then that's enough. I was paralyzed too. We were supposed to be in two different places at once. A screening 425 Lafayette at 3 of Yoko's "Fly" and John's "Apotheosis"—a champagne boat party by Gregory for his departure Queen Elizabeth II at 3 pier 92 & 52nd Street. Simone Swan was going too. I don't know why. The stewards always like Gregory. I thought of stowing away. I certainly wanted to be at the party. But what if Yoko had arranged her screening just for me? Unlikely. But still. We might well arsk. Didju cough up those icecubes out of your nose onely for us? And besigns I had spent myself many socials with Jog and Yokel beginning June something hover at Allen Klein's wife's birthday parting and pool dunking down at Riverdale where Andy David Gregory George Henry Howard Helen Jack Jerry Jonas Jane Jill Viva Michel Shirley cetera was all filming each other and recording one another's recordings of each and others excepting me and Gregory who said we were the only peoples there who didn't have something. We were the only ones who just came by ourselves. We won't have any mementos. I didn't even want the polaroid Andy took of me between Yoko and John. I told Andy he could keep it for his own album. And I didn't get the one I really wanted sitting between Jerry and Gregory that David took. David had a colored polaroid. Jonas had an old bolex. Shirley had her video stuff. Howard had Fred's nikon because Fred couldn't come. Andy had everything. The girls in the house overlooking the party had binoculars. Henry Geldzahler had a gray beard and a cowboy hat. Lindsay had royal blue boots made up in London with appliqued butterflies. George Segal had his wife and daughter. Viva had her baby. Jane Forth had a pregnancy. Jack Nicholson had Jane's roommate. The Kleins have a Jewish maditerranean house on the Hudson. Across the river from Jerome Robbins. I like Jerry Rubin a lot. He's short and smart and he said he likes me too. I ran up to him and appreciated openly so I realized he must be a hero. The revolution goes away for the summer so people go to parties instead. He said he's never been at such a rich place. Someone told Gregory he shouldn't be walking around the living room in his underpants. Gregory said the decor was trashy and all the desserts had gelatin in them. Somebody said the servants were all Spanish Black or Japanese. Shirley Clarke and Viva said they had an awful time but they enjoyed it very much back at the Chelsea looking at the videos. I watched me and Yoko embracing after two years and me giving Yoko the lesbian chauvinist once over I wouldn't have known I did that. Shirley told me they're leading this double life: one that's real and one of the tape of the life. They even videotaped their own arrest a few months ago. Shirley was feeding herself lines such as "take *me* to jail, don't take *her*" (reference for cops to Viva's baby back at the hotel). I liked both the video and the party except for the pool wasn't too much fun because it wasn't forbidden. Gregory and my son fooled around in a floating chair under a plastic bubble. I wore my new happy underwear. Viva saw me from the second floor changing her baby. Later she asked me to tell someone how to collapse her carriage, as though I should remember things like that. I think Viva's terrific anyway. She figures we're living in a world of fools so why take it seriously. She says the one thing she learned from Andy is never to take anything seriously, make it all up, always bear in mind never to give a straight answer. A friend in Teaneck who had never seen her was amazd at her weird beautiful looks, like a Garbo gone crazy. I wish I was married to her I wouldn't have to make up any of my own lines or even give her the credit. That was how Joyce got "Finnegan's Wake" from his daughter Lucia, by keeping her in the house. I called Viva to bring herself and everybody and the videos to the event I arranged on board the Queen Elizabeth II June 24 at 3 p. m. to unite my two conflicting appointments. You have to decide what you want ultimately to happen. I wanted to see Yoko's and John's films at Gregory's champagne party on the Queen Elizabeth. I didn't even try to alter the time of the sailing. I called David. The mindstorm occurred at about noon or so. He thought it was fabulous and funny but it would never happen. I called Gregory. He was packing. Hysterical. Yes yes, wonderful, he would contact the steamship company. I called Lindsay at the Abkco office. She called Dan Richter. Yes they could move the showing from Lafayette Street to the boat but did the boat have the proper equipment. I'd find out. Call Gregory back. Tell Gregory to tell the boat people we needed a 16 millimeter optical projector. Call David. He's moaning about Elsie Washington, the Life woman who couldn't come earlier or later than 3 and now nobody knew where she was so she'd be going to Lafayette and wouldn't know about the boat. I can't think about Elsie. I wanted to think the screening was just for me. David says me and Gregory are crazy. It's wonderful. Call Diane at The Voice. Tell Diane to call Fred. Tell Fred to tell Howard. Tell David to call Andy. Tell everybody. Call the Pentagon It's on! The steamship company says yes and they have the proper projector and a 500-seat theatre and the captain would like to entertain us beforehand in the Conference Room on the Quarter Deck Far fucking out! And I don't even have a brownie. It was an exquisite disaster. John and Yoko didn't show up. Simone didn't know where to go. Elsie from Life was probably wandering around Lafayette Street. Viva and her baby were thrown out of the Conference Room. David didn't take a polaroid of me and Gregory as he promised. Gregory wouldn't introduce his mother to anybody. Gregory didn't provide champagne. Gregory will hate David for sending a polaroid of him and his mother to Gay. Dan was furious because the ship censored the showing of Yoko's "Fly" because the PR man said they couldn't have a fly crawling on the heroine's vagina. Nobody understood John's "Apotheosis" which is all about snow. David said I talked and drank through the movie and didn't even watch. The ship's piano tuner interrupted the concert I was giving doing my splendid to entertain a most deserting group. And bemeantimes every famous important personage and agency in the broad world was appearing to see Yoko and John who were screwing back at the Plaza I hope. —CBS-tv. The Voice. The Times. The Gay. The Circus. The Crawdaddy. The Rolling Stone. Everybody but Elsie. Even Abbie Hoffmann! And Ornate Coleman! And Charlotte Moorman! And Barbara Loden! And Bici Hendricks! And Viva and Alexandra and Shirley and Michel and Antoine lugging their videos. And the whole great population of the floating city of Queen Elizabeth II departing 4.30 p.m. You don't have to be part of it to be for it or against it. Dan also was still put out but he was repairing a little of the damage by announcing that Yoko's "Fly" would be shown back at Lafayette immediately after John's "Apotheosis" on the boat. David told Dan it was all because of me that Yoko and

John would never be on the cover of Life. I had no idea. But I know now that I can only hope to be totally misunderstood. Anyway it was my event, so who could enjoy it totally besides me? I moved the world in an afternoon over practically nothing. And then I got to be the only of all the invited boat guests who actually saw Yoko and John the same day. Not that I knew I would. Nor that I was especially anxious, considering Yoko for me is a human being I used to know in the same dreary exciting penniless underworld of art and fucked-over women and since as I sd I'd been spending myself recently in socials Riverdales Plazas Charles Postermats Tudor Cities cetera all 10 days off & on and socks and shoes and books and flowers and patches and boxes and general summer Xmas xchange program with this beleagured but happy homosexual couple ... They came to Bici Hendrick's Flux-divorce. Bici invited me at the boat. In between the boat and the divorce I got laid at Ann Wilson's house. Ann is in Europe. Ann's ex old man came to the divorce. Bici is married 10 years to Geoff. Yoko thought they were really divorcing. I think they really were. A ritual of renewal on their 10th anniversary. Yoko told me she cried a little. I was moved myself when Bici informed me that she and Geoff came out recently. So that's why there were so many gay people there. Gay women, actually. And old Flux people. George Macunias. Jackson Maclow. Ray Johnson. Barbara and Peter Moore. Like that. And Kate Millett. It was a beautiful event. They made it difficult at first to get to the kitchen to the beer and cheese. Obstacles of tires and barbed wire. But no piano tuner to interrupt my resumed concert. Bici sang soprano or contralto. Bici looks great. So does Geoff. They had a tug of war and other ceremonies of separation. I saw the tugging only. I know that marriage and divorce are all the same. To have and to harm till death duty part. There's a spiderweb grow acrossing these old flowers. And birth and death. The tires to worm through. The barbed wire to get stuck on. The wine and beer to celebrate. And Yoko writing in my book "the past that I remember is the past that I create now because of the necessity of the present." I forgot to tell her she was divorced that day too. "Apotheosis" on the Queen and

"Fly" on the Lafayette. Elsie showed up by the way so all was forgiven by David at least. And Dan, maybe. And Gregory doesn't matter as he's out to sea. I'm flying over his head Monday night enroute to Paris. He'll be distracted by the stewards. None of this has to make sense and if it seems funny then that's enough. Viva told me that some last piece or other was my best because it was humorous, "and that's the most important thing you know."

FILMS OUT OF FOCUS

1972-03-02

Six in the fifth place means: Persistently ill, and still does not die. Obstruction of enthusiasm. Impatience for the revolution. A telepathic coalition and a derby hat. A long sunny window over-looking all the excitement. An airplane obstacle dream. I have that sort of dream sometimes. The plane is taking off and the wing tips are squeezing through buildings and the body is just almost making it under and over sets of wires and tops of trees. This time we landed in water and the pilot stepped out of his seat in a foot of it. Then we landed on a country road and couldn't get a long enough tree clearance for the wingspread to take off. I suppose it's a political dream. I have repetitive political dreams. I suppose I had in a dream the Times in a Sunday issue print a headline on every page Lesbians are Feminists, not Homosexuals. I think the Times thought I was saying lesbians want equal consideration and coverage in gay liberation when I wasn't saying that at all. I was saying we want to be left out of the male homosexual media hype. Lesbians are not homosexuals. Lesbians are lesbians. Or gay women. There may be a couple dozen lesbian feminist newspapers which identify themselves that way.

There's at least one male gay paper, the Fag Rag, that knows it isn't or shouldn't be about lesbians. Spectre comes out of Ann Arbor identifying itself in bold type under the title Spectre as written by revolutionary lesbians. There's a new one up from Washington D.C. The Furies and similarly subtitled a lesbian/feminist monthly. The gay male papers should follow the example of their straight brothers Playboy & Esquire saying right out that they're magazines for men. The press generally should add Male to all their titles. The New York Male Times. The New York Daily Male News. The East Village Male Other. Etc. Then it would be clearer how and why a woman was appearing in its pages. If the movie going population saw the credits on the screen reading the directors' names adding in bold letters white male heterosexuals we'd understand immediately we were about to watch a political film. The Battle of Algiers in bed and at home, etc. We saw X Y & Zee and I wrote down some of the white male heterosexual dialogue: S. York speaking to M. Caine re Liz T.: she always manages to come between us. Caine to Liz: Shut up your bloody slut filthy mouth. Liz to Caine: Her whole life is a lie. York to Caine: I wish now you'd let her (Liz) die. Liz on York: I think she looks like a bag of bones. Liz on Caine: It's not easy being married to a giant. Liz to York: Would you like to go watch them? (the men playing pool). York: We should've brought our embroidery. Caine over dinner with York: You see that?—that's the first time in years I've worn a watch. That's what you've done to me. Caine to York: Do you want me to take you to dinner or do you want to cook me an egg? (at home). York to Caine: It's your wife, she's possessed. Caine to York re Liz: You should've gone straight up to her, and told her to piss off. Liz: "Michael, can't we stop all this wrangling?" Michael: "Yes, as of now, wake me at eight in the morning for some coffee."—Films out of focus.—The big bed scene is at the end and we don't see any of it but we are treated to the wonderful spectacle of Caine planting his mouth on the mouths of the two women who become the subjects of that bed scene at the end, and of course Caine beating up Liz and another scene tying up her hands and other scenes waking up naked with at least two of the women and so forth. During the movie Jane said you're sitting in the dark in your derby taking notes on Elizabeth Taylor. I said we have to get together with her. Who?—Suzannah York. Jane: That movie lesbian?—I suppose she once confided in a white male heterosexual film director about a lesbian fantasy she had when she was 15. When white male heterosexual film critics put down actresses by the way they might remember that these actresses are given their lines and told what to do by white male heterosexual directors. No woman is responsible for her own performance until she directs herself: Anyway I'm interested in the courtesies of identification. One reason I liked Dennis Altman's book "Homosexual" is that at some critical juncture he incriminated himself by issuing a Warning: "I'm a white male." When a male artist I used to know comes up to me at a Moma opening and says in greeting rather grimly and gleefully "Have you seen Clockwork Orange?" I know exactly what he means but I'm not so sure he does. These museums by the way should also assume the courtesy of political clarification: Museum of Male Modern Art, the Jewish Male Museum, etc. Then we'd know better how and why a woman was appearing in its rooms. Walking through the Matisse show with Simone Swan Simone said being seen with you everybody will think I'm a lesbian. I said listen never mind this is awful, people will think *I'm* straight. I have to be careful who I'm seen with. Also now I think we have to liberate these places from their guilty conscience tokenism. A woman's place is a ladies page in the New York Times. Or a corner of a bookstore labeled "Women." We all know that. So I don't know what to say next. If a woman does something as a "person" she's included with the men as a token. If she does something as a "woman" she's identified as a special interest group. I guess when the women take everything over the men will be tokens and special interest groups too. But at least the women will have had experience in identifying all their publications and museums and movies as works and things by women. A lot of women know that women are women and men are something else. No group of lesbians would call their paper Gay, just Gay. No lesbian thinks she's a man. Lesbians aren't homosexuals, we're lesbians. For the Times to head up my story Lesbians are Homosexuals too they're expressing naturally their male trip imagining women, and possibly especially lesbians, want to be men. If they turned it about and said Homosexuals are Lesbians Too I think they'd understand the problem. The word Homosexual is largely associated with the male. Instead of attempting to change the association we alter our terminologies. Daily. I think this is the content of my political dreams. I participated last week in a panel of lesbian mothers and thought a great deal about the terminology I heard there ... *will continue*

THE YEARLY MELLOWDRAMA

1972-10-26

I had a dream richard stayed in san francisco one day and then split for home. I had a dream two years ago I was traveling up and down highways on the coast in a freighter and richard flew up in the air and landed someplace on his back as a small doll. I didn't have a dream 10 years ago he ended on his back on a road in washington heights his eyes rolled up I ran the other direction it happened to be a nurse on her way to a hospital who hit him and I followed her over with him in her front seat unconscious and richard and me discussed it ever afterwards for six or seven years until one day I said well it was a good way to pay me back for I don't remember what besides having him and he looked at me funny and that was that. I remember his left face was black and blue and swollen for a week and that was all but everything was terrible then. It was clear that we were all living thru an ordeal. I tried to remember yesterday whether richard was hit before or after I was driving myself and hit a schoolkid dashing diagonally out from between cards in the middle of a street but we talked about that forever afterwards too. That was back in 1962 when everybody in rockland county wanted to build themselves an orgone box. I remember yvonne asking me if I was into reich and I suppose I said yes since sally was reading the murder of christ and I was in love with sally and that's the way things go and I still didn't have a mind of my own in any case. I was a stroller mommie in washington heights living in an $80 walkup near the river and across the street from the park. I would carry up one kid up on my hip and trail the other behind me screaming. I would sit in the park and do all the proper things like talking to another mommie and following the kids with my eyes when they left the sandbox and swinging them on baby swings and buying the popsicles and picking them up when they cried and putting them down when they didn't and wondring whether my mission in life was supposed to be fulfilled. I don't think I wondered that for a second. I had a dream last week I went to an important interview in heels stockings black velvet dress and my derby. I don't remember too much what I whore then except some shapeless $5 jeans to the park but I did have a red woolen dress to just above the kneecaps and it was around that time that john cage saw me in my red woolen dress at a christmas party and asked me to perform with him and david tudor a number of months hence in a thing of his called music walk and I did and I did it in my red woolen dress and for my noisemakers I brought all the trappings of my wonderful maternal existence a baby bottle a coffee can a blender a frying pan a vacuum an apron a plastic sink an egg beater a beater beater and a toy dog on wheels that barked like a duck when I pulled it along by its string. I had a ladder on stage too. I had all this junk and john and david had only their minimum daily requirement of sophisticated electronic equipment and a handful of three by fours containing the brilliant and elegantly scripted hieroglyphics of instructions from the godhead: the wise decrees of chance and indeterminacy. I had gone to all this trouble too. I had come in face to a rehearsal with a bunch of about 45 of these cards clutched in my nervous little fist, each one explaining to myself how I should do such and such an action like scrubbing out my baby bottle at a very certain time and for just so long during the course of the 10 specified minutes of the piece, the result of some very fancy calculations involving the tossing of coins and an immaculate collection of topological transparencies that john called a score, but at the rehearsal I dropped all these cards of instructions in some of my domestic water and the ink was blurred and whatever wasn't blurred was dirty and I said to myself shit why should I bother with these cards anyway I'll just plant my junk around the stage and set my stopwatch so I know when we're beginning and when we're ending and whenever I feel like it I'll go here and there and tinker around with my junk and that's what I did in my red woolen dress. I remember john looking quite skeptically at me just before the performance but he didn't say anything and I didn't tell him how heretical I planned to be either. I suppose at that time if you weren't up in rockland county building yr orgone box you were training to deliver up yr ego to the elements by obeying john cage and I really wanted to and I appreciated the orgone business too but no matter what anybody else said my life was conforming to its own internal chaos, it was out of my control to follow any directions from anywhere, much less from myself, so naturally I experienced my better and better orgasms completely by chance and naturally I couldn't do anything on stage that wasn't basically like my life and that was purely by chance according to the whims of the moment confined to my wonderful maternal existence I didn't have much choice as it were but within that choice or chance I was always dropping my papers in the domestic waters and deciding to do something else because of that or something else. I was trying to remember right now whether I had that ladder on stage because around that time richard had fallen off a ladder at marcia marcus's house or not but I don't know I do know I didn't own a ladder myself so it isn't clear why I insisted on the ladder unless me and my kids were all into hanging and falling off things in which case any elevated property would've been suitable to demonstrate one important aspect of my life and a ladder happened to be handy at the theatre as I said I don't know because I didn't know anything at the time I didn't make any connections whatsoever because I was completely unconscious. I didn't put it all together—me at parties hanging from pipes, richard on the street on his back, richard falling off a ladder, richard climbing rocks and cliffs and daring me to be concerned, winnie falling off a slide on her chin her eyes rolling up and me running in the other direction and me at a party falling into a skylight and losing a black heel to the floor below I don't have to *try* and remember and although I wasn't making any special connections I knew it was all terrible. I had a call yesterday from richard from caspar california. I'm organizing his trip by remote control. Three weeks ago I said tomorrow you're going to seattle and that next day I drove him to hudson's for 2 shirts one pants one nabsack one shoes no nametapes and drove him to the airport and bought him a ticket and didn't have time to stop at the park so he could see his friends and bought him some French fries and gave him $55 and put him on a united and called seattle to snowshoe whose brother met him at that end the five hours later the next I heard he was standing on tall swaying ladders making $10 a day picking apples. I told danny that richard was among the last of the junior acid freaks who sit on rocks up at the park around the boathouse getting holes in their pants and I sent him to the coast to see the world and danny said if danny lived on the pacific coast he'd drop acid every day and sit on the cliff and watch the sun go down. A little man was walking down eighth street last week yelling Wake Up Wake Up,—They're Coming.—They're coming, of *course* they're coming, whoever they are, anybody can see that they're coming and so is the first frost in new england and the birches are showing in the hills the yearly mellowdrama and I want some candystriped doctor dentyns with feet and the thing in the back and there is no greater satisfaction than in everything so I don't know what was wrong about 1962. I met rosalyn drexler in washington heights in the park strolling her kid danny around and I was making $80 a month writing for art news and I was evicted from my $80 walkup so I could move into another nice tenement on houston street closer to this woman I'd fallen madly in love with and whom I was chasing around unashamedly. I was evicted and the eviction men threw out my babybook and my grandmother's old persian rug and when I was packing the remains I lost my wedding ring under my ford I think and that was a good thing too. This has many little interruptions and a kiss on both cheeks is not in disorder. All the tender pressing of the complete expression. All the exaggeration in examination. All this is that intention and some expectation. It wasn't really clear that we were living thru such an ordeal. I remember rosalyn yelling at sherman out her window and I remember rosalyn was said to've punched Sherman in the nose, and I remember rosalyn coming over to see me with a huge bottle of cheap chianti and I remember her kid danny beating up richard in the sandbox. I remember the sandbox thing but I don't know if that really happened I might've dreamed it and it I did it was because danny was more aggressive than richard and he probably didn't fall off ladders and I suppose that by now he's a basketball and track champ and I hope he is and for myself it was a pleasure putting richard on the plane for seattle carrying a beatup copy held together by a rubberband of the electrickoolaidacidtest he received as a gift from an elderly freak in the park. Naturally whenever the children are involved there is always a little trauma. By remote control talking on the phone to caspar california I hoped richard would spend more than one day in san francisco as I dreamed he wouldn't and he would go to the golden gate and sit around on some new kinds of rocks in that place there and then san diego and pauline isn't it amazing he's just 14 and I like the whole thing. The great fabrication of origins and imitations. Few are called and many are poisoned. Possibly the new business that began to come into being after 1962 or sometime is the business of connections as we gradually lost interest in building orgone boxes in rockland county and the study of delivering up yr ego to the elements by obeying john cage we azserted our consciousness in connections just yesterday a letter from snowshoe saying she hitchhiked back to seattle from caspar having left richard off there she immediately met a joe johnston for her traveling companion you know richard has been using his mother's last name and why 1962? Because as I just this second realized last week a susan I know told me that a man at the voice said I been writing for this paper since 1962 and that isn't true it was 1959 and I did it out of washington heights while everybody was screaming and looking at the box and eating tuna fish and falling and getting hit and generally going crazy including being unsuccessfully in love. I could get very involved trying to prove something and jane is sabotaging the argument with oreos.

DELITISM, STARDUMB, & LEADERSHIT

1972-12-14

On Saturday December 16 beginning 9:30 a.m. at McMillan Theatre of Columbia University 116th st. and Broadway will commence a conference for women only called A Feminist Lesbian Dialogue: Is the Sexual Political?—This is an unpaid political announcement. I thought up the idea a few centuries ago and then asked a couple of columbia women if they'd help launch the thing and locate the spaces for it and we met over orange juice & vodka one sunday at noon at max's which wasn't officially open and then we called a meeting which caused instant widespread agitation and dissatisfaction since the entire dyke community coast to coast was not invited. I think basically there was a misunderstanding as to the nature of the meeting that we were meeting to confer when in reality we intended to meet to organize. The intention itself it seems is always suspect in these situations. That is, who intended what, and by what prerogative, and for whom, or on whose behalf. The main thing is that when a group forms it's elitist and when it dissolves it's democratic. Since elitism is worse than the plague anyone involved in a group is asking for lots of trouble from the more indeterminate group at large until the group shows signs of internal disintegration which was true of our group immediately. I don't like groups myself. I prefer being lost in china without a friend to being found in a room with a group. I like the illusion that I'm not accountable to anybody but myself for whatever I decide to do, for example being permanently lost in china, and I feel bound and gagged by the consensus reality of a group. Nonetheless I thought this feminist lesbian thing was extremely important and that I should submit to being bound and gagged for a couple of months while the group decided all manner of things including the size and color and quality of its paper cups. That's for the dance in the evening. There is a dance and it begins at 8 and I don't even know what particular place on campus it's been designated to happen. That's how much I have to do with it by now. The group took over totally. The group isn't even a true group any more. A true group is defined by its membership boundaries. Whether it's a group of a certain permanency with a title and officials or a group like ours which was constituted for a specific function. The boundaries of this group dissolved and that was my intention. There's only one group I feel I belong to really and that's the group called women. I feel I have more in common with women than with frogs or grasshoppers or men. If I was seriously upset being lost in china I'd go looking for my bowl of soup at a nunnery. The women there may be nuns, but they're still my political peer group. I mean it doesn't matter what these women do with their bods, whether they do anything or not, since we have so much in common politically and we have the same basic equipment by which in fact we came to be identified as women who by virtue of this very equipment constitute that political group. After all, this was the revelation of feminism. We always knew we weren't frogs, but it was never clear that we weren't men. We were all one group and we were called *man kind*. Some women are beginning to wonder now if we don't actually have more in common with such specious as crustaceans than with men. That may be an idle thought, but crustaceans and women alike are not given to erecting skyscrapers. Crustaceans and skyscrapers aside, we are now eager to delineate the boundaries of the group called women by the maintenance of a collective deviant identity as it were as it were as it was. Anyway I couldn't see organizing a conference with the entire group, it just isn't practical. I'm not a practical person particularly but I have some rudimentary knowledge of organization procedure required in the selection of paper cups. I dislike meetings for purposes other than parties and I knew dimly that a meeting of 40 or 100 women or so to determine such items as cups or any other apparently serious matters would enlarge the scope of our involvement to unbearable durations. Sadly however there is yet in our society no authentic authority in a spontaneous group. There is therefore a certain tacit permission accorded any organizational group under the auspices of its known establishments, i.e. NOW, or Radical Feminists, which is currently organizing a conference on Marriage. Any ad hoc alliance is automatically elitist. It's an insult to choose yer own friends. I don't know how important all of this is. I have a rather theatrical orientation to life. In my theatre days I received numerous invitations from people to attend their events or whatever they called them. Somebody obviously would have an idea for doing something and then often as not they would ask other people to collaborate on it and then finally they would invite the population at large to come and observe and/or participate in the results. We could have hundreds of these conferences. The reaction from certain elements of the dyke community seemed to be that this was the only conference in the world that there ever was or would be. Not only is this not the ultimate conference but its actual occurrence will be as illusory as every other insomuch as the feminist/lesbian revolution is an ongoing conference and that any particular conference merely represents a kind of formal acknowledgment of a general consciousness. The theatre parallel may be insensitive, considering the global moral issues that seem to be at stake, and the emotional investment in revolution, in which context an event is more than an evening's entertainment, an event concerning issues about which each of us is an expert. The leadership problem in the movement may be second to none, and it's related to the credibility of static or spontaneous groups. As would be expected most more or less permanent (static) groups defer to an elected leadership. Such groups, having a hierarchial structural affinity with the basic institutions of oppression, are well qualified to attack these very institutions with social and legislative reform. The leadership problem is mobilized around the conflict between the essential ideological rejection of authority and the necessity of getting things done, as well as all psychological vestiges of conditioned dependencies on authoritative leadership. The praxis of the woman's movement has devolved upon process as opposed to product, on collectivism as distinct from hierarchic forms of engagement. The consciousness raising group is a leaderless structure par excellence. These structures and the revelation of feminism, that we have a common problem and that is in being women, make sensible reflections of each other. The anxiety generated over any incipient leadership springs I think from the threat such leadership may be seen to pose to our common political condition which transcends our old individual sense of worthlessness. That is, leadership threatens our solidarity by triggering old responses of worthlessness in relation to the very real oppression of static appointed elected assumed leadership in the real world of male authority. At the bottom the problem in all the worlds is distinguishing between authentic and inauthentic authority. The authority of any authority person in the world in which we grew up is granted by arbitrary social definition rather than on the basis of any real expertise that a person may possess. As Adrienne Rich says in this essay I just read in the New York Review of Books "... authority derives from a person's status—father, teacher, boss, lawgiver—rather than from his personal qualities." She's talking about the family and the patriarchy, and she makes the all important point that the sacredness of this institution—"sacred in the sense that it is heresy to question its value—relieves the titular head of it from any real necessity to justify his behavior." It has been in fact by *this* system that we all came to feminism as worthless individuals militantly aligned against authority. Thus the failure to distinguish between spontaneous leadership and static authority is an understandable one. Some feminists, specifically two lesbian/feminists that I know of, Martha Shelley and Rita Mae Brown, have tried to define the difference between stardom and leadership without projecting the possible conditions of leadership. Besides that, a star is not necessarily not a leader and vice versa, although the distinction they've brought to attention is a valuable consideration. Anyway inherent in the distrust of leadership is the automatic association of leadership with domination. No doubt the central characteristic of authentic leadership is the relinquishing of the impulse to dominate others, but this is not a quality of leadership that we've been exposed to. To lead and not to dominate seem like contradictions in terms. Yet the women's movement has been productive. I mentioned the reform type organizations, and I'm not disparaging them either. To move against the enemy utilizing the familiar organizational arrangements of the enemy is not an ineffective strategy. It's one front, rear guard or whatever. But there've been other kinds of products in the movement and I think these are the source of the greatest agony. Given as we are to process primarily, when it looks like there may be a product, the perpetrators become deviants to the tacit or overtly acknowledged leaderless underpinning of the movement. Thus one might be attempting to lead and to deny that one is doing so at the same time. A product somehow always involves identity and identity can mean status and prestige and status and prestige accruing to any particular women make other women feel worthless (again). Because the word reaches *other* women through the media and the media is male and the male media creates *stars*. A star is a certain type of appointed authority. A given position. A constant identity achieved by a particular recognized accomplishment. Another static assumed situation in other words. I need hardly mention the continuous crisis in the woman's movement between the individuals and the group over the publication of every woman's book. Possibly the most feared product of all. The next conference should be called Power Money and Fame in the woman's movement, subtitled Confessions of Some Amerikan Woman Eaters. Anyhow the worst thing about a book is that it's a solo operation, an indefensible crime. It's also a class trip, it means you finished high school and your parents were skilled laborers and you weren't born in the tennessee appalachians. But I have more to say about this dilemma another time. I want to go on making my pointless abstractions about leadership. I can't be very specific because I don't know myself how to define or identify authentic authority, I suspect in fact that if we could we'd be making a familiar brief for the old legitimate types of authority and I think we desperately need some revolutionary forms of assertion that slip in and out of process like an eel that might suddenly and unaccountably *know* a way upstream that hadn't occurred to the others who follow along for an hour or two until that particular mission is accomplished. A person who's a source of energy and initiative in a project might be considered a natural leader and that might mean for an hour. Sometimes it's a rare minute. And it isn't necessarily Charisma. We are very often taken in by non productive charmisma, in the vacuum between static authority and spontaneous leadership. All organizations tend to move in the direction of closure—hierarchical forms which transmit information through channels that run in a linear direction, from head to mass. Revolutionary structures stop short in their own organiza-linear direction, from head to chinese revolutions getting stuck at levels of static leadership. Heads or heroes replacing old heads. Positional authority replaced by charismatic authority. When the charism fails the tendency is to regress into authoritarian modes of directing energy. A proper leader does not lead. I follow the thought of somebody because it interests me. I lead myself to china to get lost. I follow myself one day to columbia to talk about lesbian feminism.

I submit to being bound and gagged for a couple of months while the group decides all manner of things including the size color & quality of its paper cups. I watch while the group takes over. I become a part of an elitist spontaneous group which shows almost immediate signs of internal disintegration. I watch while my own original idea turns into the bidding of a finally enormous group. I watch myself sometimes try to control events. I watch others on other days try to control the same or other events. I hear reports of widespread agitation and dissatisfaction. I look forward to being an irresponsible individual again, not accountable to anybody but myself.

LADY MACBETH WITH A RUBBER DAGGER

1973-06-14

i was saying i arrived in albuquerque and that's where i am now after agnes martin in the desert which is a very big subject i intend to tell later possibly a lot later. i will say i mentioned to agnes i'd been doing some of this tv stuff on the coast to which she muttered that's an entertainment medium and added conclusively you're being exploited. the next day i believe she gave me permission to do anything once. whether she did or not she would certainly say you can't get away from doing what you have to do and that could include being exploited. i'm not sure in any event what being exploited means unless it's slave or indentured labor and although i recognize such labor done voluntarily through ideas of conditioned necessity i like to imagine that most of our friends are exploiting those who exploit them and in that spirit of eat and be eaten i approach the media. actually i believe i approach this madness thinking that if there's any exploiting to be done i'm the one who's going to do it in order to offset the obvious fact that it's basically their show which is probably what agnes meant. anyway sometimes you have to saturate yourself in a basically bad thing before you find out you don't want to do it. some people never stop trying. hope springs eternal even in the context of total illusion the announcer himself might say we'll be right back after i go offstage and kill myself while i still have the chance. i felt that way myself for a moment out at berkeley i was talking to a big mixed crowd in the university museum the night of may 22 when suddenly a riot developed and i didn't leave the stage to kill myself but I covered my eyes to shut out the scene. i hate violence i provoke five or six women were carrying a male student bodily out of the area. the rest of the people were protesting and demonstrating their approval or condemnation of this action and some women toward the back were physically confronting other males refusing to leave. i told agnes about this event and she seemed to enjoy it greatly. i don't know why. i don't see how it was any better than doing my own violence by losing my temper at sarah lawrence last month and i told agnes that story too but that one she disapproved of. i disagreed and said i did the correct thing at sarah lawrence since i did my own dirty work which was an artful clap of thunder followed by a disappearance. at berkeley i issued an order more or less and then shrank from the results. the same thing could've happened at sarah lawrence however, now i realize. the order was the same. at some point i told the males to leave and in both cases they wouldn't but at berkeley the women wouldn't tolerate their presence for a second longer than the issuance of the order and at sarah lawrence the women haven't questioned apparently the existence of boys in their women's studies program so naturally, they wouldn't think of throwing them out even when or especially not when commanded to do so by an outsider. the situation at berkeley is that berkeley loves riots anyway. i guess i knew that but i thought it would be a basically apolitical evening since the place was museum and the subject was art and the speaker a writer and in fact the atmosphere was congenial for some time but i hadn't counted on the potential effect of a group of radical women who were there who probably could care less about art or museums or writing and who eventually as i might've predicted asked or challenged why i was talking all this about art and not politics to which i replied i thought i was in fact getting some politics in there but it didn't matter they weren't satisfied with the art rap at all even though i was offering such significant critical remarks as how i happened to know mark di suvero and how i once posed for larry rivers as a moon woman and how the artists never forgave me for finding their lives more interesting than their art and how clive barnes once said he would bury yvonne rainer and stuff like that it was a thoroughly enjoyable evening but i had to deal with the radical women and i did i dealt completely by capitulating to their point of view as soon as they spoke up since i agree with them anyway and i didn't mind shifting gear myself into the exclusively political but that meant that both the boys and the boy minded women which tends to include most art women were bent out of shape and the hall polarized as a basically apolitical evening in the congenial atmosphere of art turned into a normal berkeley riot. i aligned myself unequivocably with the radical women even though i know i have to relinquish politics in order to pursue writing. when certain women protested the violent action of other women ejecting the boys i said we i said we as though i was a sudden multitude we support all violence by women employed to define any space that we decide to call our own when the subject is women and a woman is presiding. i said anyhow this was my happening and the audience and/or participants in any happening always honored the directions of the artist. red rover red rover let everybody with lavender boots come over and that's what happened more or less and we went on with feminism and i suppose most of the boy minded art women left along with the boys. i wasn't happy however i mentioned to little effect that the evening before in san francisco at some auditorium i forget where but sponsored by d.o.b. had been exclusively and profitably and successfully political and i thought to myself all along i was as usual strung out between political women who have no use for the artist and artists who hate politics deluded by some floating individuals who love you no matter what and concerned that the woman who invited you might find her job in jeopardy and deeply puzzled over the advisability of leaving yr cardboard house in the woods to encourage such confusion and distraction i guess here i could quote ti-grace who told me once i always say one should attend to quality and charity begins at home not many of us seem to yearn for the security of the very things we deny. can we stop whatever it was we promised we'd always do and do something else can we can't get away from what we have to do i envied agnes her unequivocal artists evening at pasadena two nights before i was down in l.a. and had known she was going to be speaking out in pasadena at the museum there coming in from the desert to speak while her retrospective of paintings was being shown there so i went and i saw how it could be just being an artist you don't have to answer to anybody not even artists you just have to be yourself and that makes life simpler. snowshoe went with me and she said i'll bet that met everybody's expectations of hearing a sensitive artist coming out from the desert to show her insides. she also thought she was a casualty but who isn't. she also thought she wasn't a rockicrucian and i said aw c'mon she's a painter and she lives alone and she isn't young. later looking at the paintings s. noted her birthdate 1912 and she backed off surprised oh i guess i was being inconsiderate she's a little old to be involved in rock'n'roll. a week later in the desert i mentioned movements to agnes and the problem with people and she said that's the trouble with movements. you always have people you don't want. that's you and me if we go around being a movement. we all tend to be mutually obnoxious to each other from that point of view you might as well talk to these radio and tv people and not expose yourself live to anybody for whom you're the people they don't want. who wants anybody anyway nobody wants anybody but themselves and that may be why we should just go around as artists you have to pretend to be something besides yourself artist isn't such a bad front movements are too involved with other people. every political woman is a movement unto herself, and that's why we have this thing called a movement, because so many women are now speaking for themselves and there's so much general agreement that this should be so, but somehow ironically speaking for yourself tends to threaten other women's potential ef[...]ve sense of themselves and this is particularly true when you appear to be speaking for other people besides yourself which you do inevitably when you speak politically since politics involves groups you can't help it you are speaking for the group you've defined or identified as the group you align yourself with politically which in the case of feminism happens to be women. then what is the problem. we know already the chief problem and that is that most women still don't identify themselves as a group called women the problem within the movement itself is as agnes said that every movement has people you don't want. the individual and the group are incompatible. you can't apparently speak for yourself and for other people too and get away with it. i handled the problem beautifully in l.a. by doing a janis i talked in this church auditorium in between swigs from a pint of whiskey i was so smashed by the time i began and ended i don't remember a thing. they kept me waiting two hours while their local singers did extended numbers so i felt i didn't owe the situation much anyhow. and it served me right i suppose for swinging into l.a. imagining i'd have the opportunity to let the whole city know how unkindly the lesbians of amerika take to the idea of a woman masquerading as a woman (lesbian) going around stirring up a witches cauldron (she calls herself a witch too) of hatred within the movement in the name of sisterhood and then returning home to her old man in the east where her game was called a long time ago her throat was serpent, but the words she spake/ came as though bubbling honey, for love's sake, my sister was a hood, and powerful. get off my back aphrodite. i never liked that position anyway. "i am a monster and i am proud"—that alarms me (atkinson) she seems to be able to handle inconsistencies quite well and quite belligerently. you could even find in the speech she made out there that altho' she lives with a man she's thrashing women who work with men. what these women need is a little zen in their politics and a little acid in their tea. etcetera. i didn't need to worry. they've got her number out there too. they've got mine too. hopefully they now see me as a writer masquerading as a movement. personally i love vanguarditis. it commas and goes. and these permanent installations never last long. there's a beautiful beautiful field/ far away in a land that is fair/ happy landings to you amelia earhart/ farewell to you first lady of the air. the best development in the west was that b. friedan was following me around plugging my book by telling the papers how awful it is. ti-grace says she owes betty a debt of gratitude too for keeping her alive when nobody else would. lady macbeth with a rubber dagger. don't follow leaders/ watch the parking meters. the same characters keep appearing on stage in different costumes. you might as well talk to these radio tv people & not expose yrself live to anybody for whom you're the people they don't want. it's a mistake feeling wanted too. wanted or unwanted is a distraction from being yourself. then when you give up and realize it is a distraction and you don't need to worry abt yrself you might have a surprising experience. i flew to l.a. may 23 disoriented by berkeley no sleep etc. my stuff bag didn't accompany my flight etc. was whisked off right away to radio kpfk shown into a small studio seated between two charming women one of whom produced a large jug of cheap red wine and a photog from l.a. free press climbed under the table wedged herself into small triangular space to shoot pitchures at me directly across the table i though o boy or oh girl i'm not gonna make this one but no sooner were the mikes adjusted & the juice turned on that i felt as tho i'd climbed into a crockpit of a lear jet with these three women we just went zooming off red wine and all and it was the most intelligent dynamic interview media situation i'd been engaged in and this didn't raise my confidence at all, it was merely one surprisingly good experience. after that there was mark bragg cbs who was as bad as his name, there was one tony gilbert of nbc monitor made up like a real woman white boots miniskirt deep peasant blouse cleavage livid lipstick dyed dark corkscrew curls deep sexy voice wanted to know had i ever been to a shrink and had there been any medical research on lesbianism, there was lunch at the brown derby with a human behavior magazine woman good professional aggressive smart woman who wanted to talk about men mostly what else, there was phyllis somebody of a paper called the staff who just wanted to hang around i guess who said she'd never had a lesbian experience mostly she thought through lack of offers and i took her out to dinner, there was one jack anderson of kioi who said tell me the things that've happened that bore you that you don't want to talk about and i was too bored to say and who later took me on a tour of the playboy club down the block, there was the prize situation kgoe in westlake an hour with one joe gazin in a sort of lord fauntleroy sailing outfit setting it up by telling his listeners he was sure there'd be a lot of opposition and a lot of women would take offense at what i'd have to say and find it totally repulsive and then trying to make it seem fair at the same time by adding i'm just a man and you people may have some other ideas and later accusing me of not being tolerant of the views of a caller (who happened to be hysterical) as tho anybody was ever tolerant of lesbians and so on and there was a guy earlier or the next day looked like a skier surfer cerulean blue eyes was actually so respectful and intelligent and prepared that i've forgotten his name and his station but i exploited him very well. everything you do is okay and if you say you shouldn't've done that that's okay too. i also did all the things you don't get morally upset about. the brown derby is a sexy place for lunch and i ate at the source and the villa frascati and the aware inn and the silver spoon in duvall and la paloma in encinitas and la cocita in taos and agnes took jane and me to la placita in albuquerque after she drove us out of her desert. also i stayed in the chateau marmont in l.a. i recommend for hugeness and fantasy and the company of weird rock hollywood types. also in seattle i saw a margaret rutherford flick and in berkeley i met laura x of the women's history library and i saw kate who came to a gig i did in s.f. and whose friend maria del drago gave me a pot of white flowers and i met a woman rebecca boone who chauffeured me in her mazda all over the place like a maniac i liked it a lot and i saw lin and pauline in san diego, that's it, friends and restaurants and a little zen in our politics a little acid in our tea, could be all we need. the poof is in the putting.

AGNES MARTIN: SURRENDER & SOLITUDE

1973-09-13

going to see agnes martin in the desert came to seem to me like a pilgrimage and i don't see why not. a pilgrimage is a long, weary journey, as to a shrine. a shrine is a tomb of a saint or other sacred person. none of these words may apply to any contemporary venture, at best perhaps they have exotic unreal connotations, but agnes martin is a spiritual woman and she isn't easy to find. unless you happen to be in los angeles when she's speaking at the pasadena museum, which was just my luck last month while passing down the coast. i was mildly disappointed since i wanted her to be as hard to find as I'd been told she was and i guess the last place i expected to see her first since she disappeared from civilization was in the civilization of a museum. yet i was relieved in a way, just to see that she was alive for one thing, and to have the opportunity to see how she felt about me before i made so bold as to trek into her wilderness with only a oneway advance telegram to recommend my arrival. i was disappointed in general to hear that agnes had been emerging at all. she has in fact made six museum appearances this past year, and she told me she flew to germany recently to negotiate the sale of some prints, it seemed therefore that i'd be visiting somebody who was just very inaccessible and not a recluse from civilization, nonetheless she is basically a recluse and she always has been thus it doesn't matter now any more than before how far you got to see her unless you like to travel and see deserted places. i used to see agnes in her loft on the battery and i don't know if she's any different now than she was then and she left new york in 1967. i think if anybody's different it's me and although i thought she was very special then i doubt that i heard what she had to tell me. i was just awed to be in her presence. i knew she was one of the great women. it was a pleasure finding a great woman in new york city during the terrible time of the '60s during every terrible decade it's a pleasure finding a great woman. a great woman may be a woman more interested in herself than in anything else. one way you knew agnes martin was great was because she lived decisively alone and that this was an active irrevocable choice and because she put very little stock in people at all and another way you knew she was great was because her paintings were. i know agnes would say the work is completely apart from the person and i have no quarrel with that myself but i see the work and the person as indissoluble too. my earliest memory of agnes is of her work alone but then a little later on i saw agnes and her work together and in fact i rarely saw them apart since whenever i went to her loft almost always as i remember she showed me her paintings and sometimes her drawings too and so for me agnes was agnes the painter although i understand her detachment. her paintings are not about the world and i suppose her paintings paint themselves and in this sense she has nothing to do with it. i think it was 1964 when i stopped in at the elkon gallery and saw all these six by six foot paintings washed out whites and tans crossed by close vertical and horizontal lines muted and irregularly perfect and i called up dick bellamy and said do you know this woman agnes martin why aren't you showing her i thought at that time that if anybody good was around he was supposed to be showing them but of course he knew her work and he wasn't showing her elkon was anyway that was my introduction to the work of agnes martin. a little later on either by design or accident i was knocking on her door to review her most recent show for art news and that was how i met her. already i thought her paintings were beautiful and i wanted to meet the artist. i wasn't the least bit disappointed but socially possibly i was more awkward than she was so i wonder how we impressed each other. her hair was long then and she had lots of it and when i came in it was all loose and she was busying herself putting it back or up and sort of apologizing for being in some disarray. i know we had tea and i looked at her paintings but i don't know what else. looking at agnes's paintings with agnes was a quiet concentrated ceremonious ritual. there was a very certain distance she traversed from the point in her loft where the paintings were stashed to the spot right next to the door where she showed them. one by one without any hurry or hesitation she would carry them from one place to another, back and forth, and when she reached the showing place next to the door there would be a certain gesture of hiking the work with her foot under the canvas up into position on the nails sticking out of the wall. then she would sit down next to you and contemplate the work with you and wait as i imagined for you to speak your thoughts. i can't imagine what i ever said if anything. i know we discussed the titles. i think very often she wanted to know if some particular title or other was appropriate but i'm not sure. i liked them all myself. desert. islands. mountain. blue flower. hill. starlight. ocean water. leaf. untitled. i liked them all. i thought i could see what they were even though everything was a graph. i used to say to people there was this painter painting mystical geometries as though nobody else had thought of that. nature paintings ruled by the horizontal line or was it vertical. when she was young she painted the mountains as they were or as we suppose we see them or anyway the way you see them at the washington square outdoor art show. in the desert agnes told me she could see in nature there weren't any *real* verticals or real horizontals and right then she gave up nature. in the desert there weren't any paintings at all. there was a rectangular pit maybe six feet deep and 15 feet from corner to corner next to her little adobe that she said was the foundation for a studio. she abandoned new york and painting both when she left in '67 and now she is beginning to begin again. it isn't altogether clear why she left new york and why she stopped painting but if you heard the story it's the sort of story you accept and understand without any explanations. leaving new york has become as much a ritual exodus as going to new york is a ritual initiation. people said oh agnes martin left in a dodge pickup, and nobody knows where she went, or you'd hear vague reports that she ended up in the new mexican desert. i asked agnes how she ended up there, why she chose cuba, and she said she saw these mountains on this road leading northward into cuba in her minds eye in new york and that was how come. i was amazed to find the place. i sent a telegram as i said but i never made the 6 a.m. bus out of albuquerque that i declared i would, the reason being that jane was flying in from new york and arriving 11 a.m. and i didn't know that till after i sent the telegram and i didn't send another because i didn't want to make any more declarations. anyway about 3 p.m. three women of albuquerque drove us north toward cuba where i enquired in the postoffice if they knew where agnes lived. they said no but a man down the road did. down the road the man's daughter explained carefully and i thought it sounded pretty clear. basically she said there was a gate a dry river bed and a little forest. i don't see gates dry river beds or little forests very often so i heard it all in the singular. i'm still certain she said it that way too. well there were lots of gates and dry river beds and little forests. first you had to drive some few miles out of cuba way off the main drag if you could call the road through cuba that. the gate the man's daughter mentioned was obvious enough, an impressive barbed wire gate the sort you have to get out and unhinge and swing away for the car to pass and then rehinge again. then we were on a soft red clay road. then we crossed the dry river bed. then there was a little forest, midget gnarled trees of some sort. then i expected to see agnes's adobe. but what there was was another gate. i didn't think we should go through it but we did because there wasn't any other place to go in order to reach a dwelling unless you went careening off into the sage and the arroyas, those dry river beds in the form of drastic looking jagged ditches that snake around all over the place through those parts. so we went on and everything began to look like a dry river bed and a forest. i asked one of the albuquerque women what we were driving through actually. she said it was a short grass prairie with incursion of sonoran desert species running into pinon-juniper forest. that sounded good. i liked being there and all too, but the apprehension was mounting, especially when there was not only a third gate but a fork or a choice of going off or on the same road unimpeded by a gate.

moreover we had passed the half eaten carcass of a cow right along the side of the road and that seemed to create an adage in my mind that when you see a dead cow you should turn back. besides i had the feeling we were within a clods throw of agnes's adobe but some part of my head said we were going to die in the desert. anyway we were all neurotically consuming a bag of nectarines and i was about to die laughing. i thought i'd never be able to travel in the desert with lucia since we were both particularly dying laughing. i said we should turn back. it was quite a few miles inching back over the soft clay bumpy road and reopening the gates and closing them behind us and wondering where the hell agnes was. back on the macadam we went a half a mile up to a little ranch farm to ask this man and his wife if we'd been on the right series of gates river beds and forests for agnes martin and the man said yes and his wife drew diagrams in the dirt and the man gestured out across the plain and said that's her mesa, right there, as though i should be able to see it and there was a curl of smoke out of a chimney that i was missing. it was clear anyway that we had to go through that third gate where the fork was where we'd turned back so we did it again and we came to a real little sage and juniper forest and there it was a small complex of vehicles and structures that had to be agnes. agnes the classicist. classicism she says is not about people and this work is not about the world. classicists are people that look out with their back to the world. it represents something that isn't possible in the world. It's as unsubjective as possible. the classic is cool. it is cool because it is impersonal and detached. if a person goes walking in the mountains that is not detached and impersonal she's just looking back. to a detached person the complication of the involved life is like chaos. if you don't like the chaos you're a classicist. if you like it you're a romanticist. painting is not about ideas or personal emotion. painting the desert in her head. the horizontal line. there's very few verticals in nature. and there she was as vertical as i remembered her which was only a week ago at the pasadena museum sitting on a chair in the middle of the stage surrounded by an overflow audience her hair short to the ears and still brown and wearing a sort of tangerine velveteen skirt to the floor with a white starched blouse slightly femme flared at the elbows and twisting a white handkerchief in her lap as though it was worry beads and my friend with me said she looked a dead ringer for gertrude stein. picasso said he was impressed by gertrude stein's physical personality and anyone might say the same of agnes martin. She's extremely handsome and she has the most brilliant twinkling blue eyes and her body is full and she's very solidly there yet shy and a little retreating at the same time. she giggles and jokes a lot and laughs at herself and i'd never seen her so solemn and formal. and i'd never seen her in a skirt or any sort of a "blouse." i could *see* she was on her best behavior. even as though it was sunday school or something. the audience too was reverent and expectant. it was a new aspect of agnes to me. although not one i wouldn't have envisioned. as i said she was for me a spiritual woman and i was awed to be in her presence and i believed whatever she said i knew she was a right person a natural woman a presence of the universe. she made pronouncements and spoke in aphorisms and she was known to go into trances and she proclaimed the future and she had no pretensions about herself except perhaps as a painter which may possibly be the subject of her intimate and abstracted speech that she's given lately in several of these museums. it's called the underlying perfection of life and almost the first thing she says is we are blinded by pride and that living the prideful life we are frustrated and lost that we cannot overcome pride because we ourselves are pride but we can witness the defeat of pride because pride is not real and cannot last, when pride is overcome we feel a sudden joy in living, the best place to witness the defeat of pride is in our work … all the time we are working and in itself … all the time in your working your self is expressed in your work in everyone's work in the work of the world we eliminate expressions of pride. her speech is 4000 words long she told me, and she memorized the whole thing. she speaks of pride, and pride, and perfection and solitude and fear and helplessness and defeat and disappointment and surrender and discipline and the necessity of all these and the necessity of the defeat of pride. besides knowing why she left new york i wanted to know why she left new york but i had no way of asking. she was glad to see me by the way. she baked an apple pie for the occasion and then when i wasn't on the 6 a.m. bus from albuquerque she was disappointed and ate some of it. i was glad she was glad to see me and i was glad we drove past the dead cow again and found her. i left jane and the three women of albuquerque in the car a discreet distance from her adobe and walked over there and hailed her and she emerged from the door beaming in dark blue work clothes very tanned or desert weathered i thought and that makes her eyes bluer and more sparkly. she was pleased i didn't bring everybody to the door at once because she wanted to change her clothes. she put on a clean shirt and pants and i explained that the three women of albuquerque were going home in case she wondered. but first we all had the apple pie and a french fish soup bouillabaisse with salmon okra and tomatoes. i was very nervous. or very high and nervously attuned to her emanations and expectations. later jane and me agreed we were afraid of her. i couldn't remember being afraid of her before so i decided i'd changed a lot. i must've been more presumptuous about myself before. or not so aware of the extraordinary presence i was in. or we were both crazy and i thought she was my peer. i don't know. i *was* in awe, but less conscious perhaps. there was the most incredible evening in '66 i think it was when i brought five or six people over to her loft and we sat around in a vague circle in a sort of a trance as though it was a seance although nobody mentioned it and there was at one point this great overhead crash i don't know what it was it wasn't thunder and lightning it might've been a skylight on the roof or even her skylight but whatever it was she didn't bat a lash she went right on talking and asking us all what sort of a wall or body of water we imagined in our minds eyes and when we saw the wall or the body of water would we cross it or could we and if so how would we do it she went right on with this exercise testing us i imagined for correct answers anyway as though nothing had happened which is her basic approach to life. nothing happens. no verticals. everything the same.

a quiet existence. not much time for other people's problems. lots of time to herself. solitude and loneliness and contentment with one self. the union of opposites without trying to do so. the friend who went with me to the pasedena talk wrote and told me the whole thing seemed much stronger now than it did at the time but what she absolutely remembers about it is that everything she said she also negated completely, and she doesn't know how she did it. she does contradict herself all the time with the most bewildering confidence. she'll say all conventional people spend 90 per cent of their time wondering is it right or wrong. what you do is right, that's it. then she'll be cato the censor and tell you how absolutely wrong you are. She'll tell me one moment that associative thinking is the basis of all our distraction and the next that i'm exceptionally lucid when i'm at the typewriter. she'll tell me i'm very prudish and priggish (and she *knows* i'm a snob), and later on she'll say i shouldn't use four letter words. she'll say she wanted to ask me something although she wasn't into winning anything and then suddenly there's an argument and it seems as though somebody has to win something if we're to proceed to the next. i think she's delighted to see people but her fear of being disappointed by people is intense. she says she talks all the time when people come in order not to know more than she wants to know. she said you mean you realized how mean we all are? she said about people who come to see her believe you me, i run em off if i don't like them, if they're inconsiderate. she said it with a little chuckle. and told about a couple who came and lived off her for two days and the woman ate a peach from their car right in front of her and didn't offer her one. she doesn't know really why people come to see her. i wasn't sure myself, being such a pilgrimage and all. i just know she's important to me. and i was very curious to see how she was living in the desert. and i still wondered why she left new york even though i knew. i didn't know how to ask but she offered a number of hints gratuitously she said i don't blame people for not being able to see the paintings, goodness knows, i have no idea why i did them myself. she said i had 10 one-man shows and i was discovered in every one of them. finally when i left town i was discovered again—discovered to be missing. she said she didn't know if she had left the world behind or the world had left her. she said she left new york because of remorse. she said that out at the edge of the canyon after we walked out through the sage to see the sunset. i didn't say anything at all. i guess it isn't necessary to clarify everything or anything. the canyon and the sunset were what seemed to matter and that didn't matter either. a glow was on us though and agnes extended what i thought must be the rarest compliment for her. she said everybody who comes is very conventional except me. it was after that that we were walking back to her adobe and she said she wanted to ask me something although she wasn't into winning anything. it was certainly a difficult moment.

AGNES MARTIN (2): OF DESERTS AND SHORES

1973-09-20

It was certainly a difficult moment I was saying I was saying that was when we walked back from the canyon and the sunset and agnes said she wanted to ask me something although she wasn't into winning anything and i knew it would be some sort of political question which would mean she would stop liking me having just said out at the canyon that everybody who comes is very conventional except me. i have no idea what she meant by the question all i can say is it concerned domination and i think whether i hadn't experienced domination or being dominating. i thought possibly she was alluding to women as role players. i had no intention of mentioning the despairing word feminism, agnes was born in 1912 and it doesn't take much ingenuity to see that she's better off in the desert throwing mud at her adobe and polishing her green truck than i am going around meeting hundreds of strange women who might have nothing more in common than electricians and philosophers but who in the name of feminism take issue with your four syllable words so that we can all be the same that is to say feminists, thus i believe i was appropriately evasive and the only remark i remember is agnes saying her sister says she believes in men women children and dogs and we left it at that although that wasn't the end of it. the thing is in any case one remains modest and gives honor to the sage who stands outside the affairs of the world. out around her adobe she pointed out the loco weed, which drives horses crazy she said. she explained how you make adobe mud bricks by filling up four rectangular sections of these open wooden frames with the mud stuff and then leaving them out to dry or bake in the sun. she talked about animals having thoughts and how she doesn't keep domestic ones any more, she doesn't want them around any more than people. what she keeps exactly is five vehicles in perfect working order and a beebee gun and a regular .22. not counting the small adobe in which she cooks and eats and possibly reads and undoubtedly muses, an open tall shedlike garage where she was parking her new shiny blue vw sports model, an outhouse, a tiny cave log room guest dwelling and a compost affair and she still sleeps in the dodge pickup or the pickup detached from the truck in which she lived for a couple of years riding all round the u.s. and canada till she found the proper mesa. when we drove away i said it didn't seem as if we were driving off a mesa, she said that's because we drove off the back end. anyway she keeps all her machines in good shape. before we woke up she polished her green truck, a '48 chevie, she said. the jeep we didn't see because she keeps it in town in case the roads've been more washed out than usual. i didn't see how we made it in in her white dodge truck returning from taos there must've been some rain and the dodge had zilch traction so i kept ditching off to the side to a standstill and somehow retreating backtracking and then racing forward as though to hit your mark meaning staying on the road as in archery if there's a wind you shoot or aim way off target in order to hit it or even boomerang yourself. after the first night there she gave us a vacation and we went to taos. i was relieved in a way since the telepathy is pretty heavy and i had had a nightmare and the scrutiny is relentless and while she completely disarms you she then flatly contradicts you and as i've indicated i was fearful of exposing what could only be a profound political disagreement between us. i read a hilton kramer review she had there of her retrospective in philadelphia and couldn't help saying the reason she doesn't have the reputation hilton kramer says she should have is because she's a woman. but agnes knows exactly who or what she is or isn't she shot back i'm not a woman and i don't care about reputations. i said well i wouldn't come to see you if you weren't a woman. she concluded the argument saying i'm not a woman, i'm a doorknob, leading a quiet existence. in taos jane thought of buying her an enamel doorknob we saw there but we brought back some cheese and syrup instead. also jane bought some eggs milk and apples and agnes said that was exactly what she needed so as concerned the food we were in perfect agreement. another safe thing was finding out more about agnes, i never asked her much before, i never seriously wondered why she was so different and a natural woman of the universe, or even why i felt close to her while knowing she had her life a lot more together. i never knew she was scottish for instance, but i didn't know how scottish i am until recently either. i think the first thing i asked her over the apple pie and french soup boubaise was where did she come from. then i asked her if she likes the bagpipes and she replied oh yes. a half a mile away. she doesn't come from scotland herself actually. she was born and grew up in saskatchewan, somehow i always thought it was vancouver. i thought vancouver was a wild uncharted territory, but i happen to be in vancouver right now and i can see how agnes couldn't possibly have come from vancouver, i never inquired what saskatchewan is but it sounds northern and wild and right for where agnes would have to come from. she's a mountaineering camping pioneering frontier type of woman whose unnatural habitats for reasons of turning out to be a painter were vertical claustrophobic cities like new york. she's climbed big mountains alone for years so i can only imagine how she felt going three hours upstate new york with me and thalia poons one summer for a little two day cook and sleep-out next to a crick river and 20 yards in from the macadam but she never mentioned what an elementary tourist trip it was. the crick was deep enough to submerge and swim a few strokes around where we camped and she seemed happy tearing off her clothes yelling at last at one with nature and doing so. it was there that she divined my future and said i would go insane again which i did. another fairly safe thing to talk about is insanity since i suppose we would both agree that nobody knows anything about it except the insane. i think it was at the very end of the summer that i did go out again and agnes and thalia were the ones who rescued me up in brewster where i abandoned my car and called them and waited for them to drive up in somebody's vw bug and didn't take the whole bottle of thorazine that agnes suggested i should but rather about 400 mcs or mgs or whatever they are. possibly agnes asked me what was wrong with me and i said i was afraid to die. yet in her wall and body of water game in which she asks people what sort of a wall you imagine or body of water and when you imagine it if you could cross it or go over it and if so how you would do it i was the one apparently who had the correct answer, at least to the wall question, and that was that the wall was transparent so naturally i could walk through it and whatever was on the other side was the same as on this, so it doesn't seem reasonable that i was afraid to die unless the game we played occurred later on and i was by that time dead or dead on the one hand and alive on the other so it didn't matter. on her mesa in the desert agnes told us the women in her family live a long time although her mother died young, at 75. she told us all about how she died, how it took two years and how happy she was when it happened, i mean how happy her mother was, and agnes's final pronouncement on death was that you go out either in terror or in ecstasy and clearly her mother was ecstatic. she said her mother was one of the little people. agnes isn't very tall herself but partly because of being full and solid of body she appears a medium height. she says at 60 your body begins to fall apart, whether she is or not it doesn't seem to cramp her style, when we emerged that first morning from the log cave guest dwelling she was standing on a ladder hurling handfuls of mud at the wall of her adobe. by little people i believe she was alluding to the fairies of old celtic scotland. the rest of what i found out about who she is or where she comes from was that an ancestor was the scottish poet who was the author of flanders fields and her father was an essayist and there weren't any painters in the family. she thinks everything happens according to destiny and i objected on grounds of social oppression which was one more instance of my political tactlessness. i was saying that my mother painted lobster pots and boats in the harbor at sunset and that her potential for being an artist or an artist's artist or an artist to herself and nothing else was undeveloped for social reasons but i was saying altogether too much. someone has to be absolutely quiet when the other holds forth agnes remarked. and she talks all the time when people come in order not to know more than she wants to know. but i was thinking some of the time how to get agnes's attention. jane had the idea that sometimes she must feel awfully heavy to herself and then i thought she hasn't had enough people respond to her humor and jane said yeah they're probably too busy at her feet. were we supposed to ask her the meaning of life questions. do people go in order to ask her the meaning of life questions. i guess they would. but she doesn't have any answers, for nobody can tell anybody something they don't already know. she says what she knows for what she knows is what she is and what that is is perfect for her and she is still on the path herself. she says one thing she has a good grip on is remorse. and that suffering is necessary for freedom from suffering. and that the wriggle of a worm is as important as the assassination of a president. and that our work is very important but that we are not important. and that what you want to do is your work and what you want to want to do is your work. and that people ask her whats going to happen in art, where is art going and she says gosh, i hope it's going to go in all directions. and that a sense of disappointment and defeat are an essential state of mind for creative work. a working through disappointment to further disappointment to defeat. what does it mean to be defeated. it means we cannot move ... but still we go on, without hope, without desire, and without dreams, then it is not i, then it is not us, then it is not conditioned response ... without hope there is hope, we go on because there is no way to stop, going on without hope and desire is discipline, going on without scheming or planning is discipline and without striving or caring is discipline ... defeated you rise to your feet like dry bones, these bones will rise again ... undefeated you will only say what has already been said ... defeated having no place to go you will await and perhaps be overtaken ... defeated, exhausted, and helpless you will perhaps go a little bit further. helplessness is very hard to bear, helplessness is blindness, in helplessness we feel as though some terrible mistake has been made, we feel cast into outer darkness as though some fatal error has been made ... feelings of loss and catastrophe cover everything and we tremble with fear and dread but when fear and dread have passed as all passions do we realize that helplessness is the most important state of mind ... lack of independence and helplessness is our most serious weakness as artists. and that's the way agnes goes on in her 4000 word speech that i heard at the pasadena museum and a few of those things she said to me and i think her critical attitude her relentless scrutiny her voices of perfection her examination of your words and deeds is all in the spirit of improving your character for otherwise why would you go such a distance to see a woman who is herself on the path of perfection which is to say to becoming most totally who she is. she said sitting in the adobe or someplace if only i could get non resistance. she understands remorse but she needs non resistance, that's clear isn't it. yet while walking seems to cover time and space in reality we are always just where we started. i went for a little walk along the rocky edge of the canyon behind her adobe and was amazed to see a tremendously long procession of small black ants in an orderly line up and down this rock facing down into the canyon some going up and some going down with a few stray dissenters or were they the lost ones. i picked up a sandstone to take back to the world. i returned to eat supper. i didn't do much else there. i did take a shot out her door with her beebee gun at a can she placed for my aim after a quick lesson in how to hold the thing i hit the can and quit while i was ahead. also i thought there was a sudden rainbow just to commemorate our visit and i said i'll bet you rarely have a rainbow here and agnes replied yes we do, all the time, it's forever raining when the sun is shining. but the last perfect double rainbow i saw was a couple of years ago in mendocino so i was in and out of her adobe ooing and ahing catching it out in the open or through one window or another watching its aspects and fading disappearing act. about 6 p.m. the wind was blowing in the canyon. by nightfall we were in bed, there isn't any electricity, and i had another nightmare. there was of course just a little bedtime story, of multiple rapes in cuba, a most dangerous part of the country apparently. but agnes had a nightmare too, she was quite indignant about it, she said she knew thoese nightmares weren't hers, and that's why she can't be around people, because she takes on their ... she picks up their ... and jane told her i needed to live among people and agnes said then i must have more pain. i could of course consider exchanging the pain for the nightmares in the desert. yet i could say like her that pain is necessary for freedom from pain. anyway if we are always just where we started there isn't anyplace to go and we might's well be where we are. i was reading recently about merlin who retreated from the world into his forest hermitage. it was said that at the sight of a crowd of people his madness breaks out anew. it was said also that his laugh was especially well known, the result of his more profound knowledge of invisible connections. agnes has this laugh or this cosmic giggle, but i wish to say she isn't any magician. she disavows magic adamantly. she hates magic and fetishes and superstition and the i ching, she says superstition is a belief in power, that there've been whole ages where art was only fetishes and that superstition is the enemy of art. she is also as a classicist as a cool artist a woman who looks out with her back to the world a painter who paints not about ideas or personal emotion but who paints the desert in her head as a classicist she is also eloquently opposed to romance and romanticism. she said she never met anybody who wasn't searching for love. she thinks this is a great mistake. she described a time of her own enslavement in this respect and how she became definitively done with it. the voices of perfection. of being alone with your self. of everything being the same. of not having any verticals. of lots of time to herself. of not much time for other peoples problems. of solitude and loneliness and contentment with one self. the union of opposites without trying to do so. a zen sort of person who never studied zen. a woman perhaps who's endured many insults, and who forgives everybody—and nobody. a woman who doesn't believe in influence unless it's you yourself following your own track. a woman it seems to me absolutely fearless of saying what she thinks. after all she doesn't depend on people. the work is what counts and the work is so fine and the people like the work so much that they pay her to live without any people. once she took a freighter around the world and someplace in india they took her off the boat and confined her in a hatch because she'd gone into a trance. no doubt the people on the boat were altogether too much. the boat in the desert is a beebee gun a .22 and five vehicles in perfect working order and i'm not without a little remorse that i went to see her myself. do we have to give honor in person to our sages standing outside the affairs of the world. or bother them with ideas of themselves that they don't have themselves and be bothered ourselves by ideas of ourselves they may have that we don't or bother at all. i don't know. in albuquerque after she drove us out and we were having lunch in la placita i asked her if she didn't think she was leading an exemplary life and once again she knocked the whole thing, oh my no, i'm a murderer, i'm a this and a that, i'm working out the hairy ape in myself, i'm just beginning, and so on, and i remembered how she leaned forward intensely in the adobe and said somewhat incredulously and you realized how mean we all are and i nodded yes, so how could i exempt her from her own conclusions about life. the work is the thing. the grid is still because the whole can be grasped by the eye and mind at once. the value she places on the known rather than the seen suggests innate ideas which she sometimes calls a memory of perfection. agnes martin: a study in the memories of perfection. "the ocean is deathless/ the islands rise and die/ quietly come, quietly go/ a silent swaying breath/ i wish the idea of time would drain/ out of my cells and leave me/ quiet even on this shore."

INSEPARABLE PARTICLES

1974-06-13

... and we were landing in portland oregon i was saying last week although even last week was a universe away from when i was landing and as much away again from when i was writing about landing and each of these activities is preceded by a tremendously long migration and i have so many other airplane stories besides landing in portland may 13 and today my ants were having a footballhuddle around some piece of honey and every breath the earth takes produces enormous changes in evolution and i still seem committed to relating the rest of portland then olympia then seattle and back to new york may 17. relating is connecting conveying transmitting conducting moving bearing relaying etc and that's what we're doing all the time. re- is an inseparable particle which means again. back. anew. against. the subject of every feminist workshop is relationships. it doesn't matter what they say they're about, they're always about relationships. and when they really take off the relating is wonderful. women may be talking about relationships but everybody just begins feeling good being together. someday as snue said we're gonna have amazon nation in canada & hopefully the indians will let us live near their land. the women most women are still living in some isolated unit of one or two approximating the model of the heterosexual institution. therefore most talking about relationships concerns pairing and how to do it. good morning, the eggs are bleeding. reaching out she fell over. pick up your arms she said. you'll need them tomorrow. there'll be oceans of talk and emotions without end. the pathology of devotion. i was saying last week i met my second connection out of new york in the chicago terminal she came up to me and introduced herself and said something right away about relating to me and i changed my seat so we took two together near the back next to a woman in an immaculate white rayon pants suit reading "dibs" and wearing earphones, i suspected she was a therapist of some sort and it turned out she was although at the moment she was getting away from her husband and children for a week and meeting a lover in portland. we talked about whether she was telling her husband or not and how that was supposed to work out, then daniel, my first connection, out of new york into chicago, walked by on his way to the lav and told me he'd been rapping since chicago with a woman who was a gestalt therapist and the thing is daniel and me had been into a heavy rap ourselves about teachers gurus therapists whatnot and then my new friend linda as i mentioned also turned out to be a therapeutic sort of person and i don't know i guess some of us learned a lot from each other on this particular plane trip so we were teaching and learning and getting high together and by the time i was landing in portland i felt like i had met my most intimate family which is now a universe away but so are my ants in their footballhuddles around their pieces of honey and the earth is breathing new enormous changes in evolution while i go on relating the rest of landing in portland then on to my official connection in olympia for a "gay conference" at evergreen state college. saying goodbye to my new intimate family in portland i was met by another who actually grabbed me up in her arms although i'd never met her before but amazon nation is very friendly that way so i felt so welcome in portland that almost immediately i went to sleep for two days. some women hug & kiss you a lot and even play with your breasts. some women give you books & other intellectual material for your work. some women send you letters. some women seem capable of forgiving you all your transgressions. some women invite you to exotic french restaurants in strange cities. after sleeping for a couple of days linda from the plane called me and asked me out to dinner where meticulous gentle hippies in white aprons gave recitations of the menu and i was coming alive. we decided we found each other attractive and would go to bed after the party back at ellie's and becky's who had met me at the airport and brought me to their house anyway the dykes of portland were coming there for a party and the next morning we were driving up to olympia where snowshoe would meet us coming down from seattle. all this relating and connecting conveying transmitting conducting moving bearing relaying etc. lots of movement and very little activity. a matter which has been thought to be important is really of slight consequence. all this energy plunging around meeting no resistance. the "real" family specializes in the formation of roles for its members rather than in the laying down of conditions for the free assumption of identity. this has been the death period. everyone died from grief. everyone then promptly woke up and grieved some more to date no one claims success in maintaining or even in defining primary relationships. the suggestion of the breakdown of existing models induces the most intense fear and makes people want to hold onto the structures they had the subject tends to be pairing but when a large group meets it begins breathing together the roles become indistinguishable even though we're talking about them. who's playing what to whom, for how long, under what conditions, where, why, and throughout all these roles there's a connection. the role that most interests me now is that of mediator, that means guiding a group in some sense and finding channels for the energy to start moving around and flowing in common directions even while we're telling all different sorts of individual stories about how we do it or want to do it or have done it and see ourselves in our stories mutually reflected in our satisfactions disappointments longings leanings leaps latitudes and love after all. the workshop of women at evergreen at 4 p.m. following some formal happenings beginning at noon was a terrific and instructive experience for me. two cars of us drove up from portland. i was driving with linda who dropped acid within a half hour of the gig. being as how i was still somewhat sleeping and due to speak formally at noon i was grateful for the contact high. ultimately as i wrote universes ago last week she turned things around more obviously and became my "healer" because she easily perceived that i was totalled from assuming one kind of role for a few hours. that such a presumption was necessary i had no doubt. at 4 p.m. about 70 or 80 women poured into a lounge where a lot of comfortable chairs had been arranged in a loose circle this was too many women. there was no need to say so. within a half hour the group sorted itself out and sifted down to a more negotiable number and also during that time the various "confrontations" took place so that by 4.30 we were ready to have a good time and exchange our stories and energies. almost always in my experience as i've seen it the initial problems are generated around the difficulty of locating a space to talk about ourselves. since this was a "gay conference" most of the women there were lesbians and or political lesbians but naturally there were a few socalled straight women there too so the first order of business is to somehow expel the "male" in our midst since most of us are interested in our muttering and doddering among ourselves. the revolution really is finding out who *we* are. and the incorporation of males into the discussion inevitably arouses the most intense hostility and resistance from women who are still angry or militant still in the process of mentally separating from the male institutions and forming a new identity thus very vulnerable to the male within as well as the male without. i do really think the revolution is about discovering new prototypes or identities of ourselves, and even when we feel more secure in these invented forms which moreover themselves keep changing we're still surrounded by the old models. thus any workshop situation is an enclave where we can feel freer to pursue the new ideas of ourselves that we're in the process of evolving, of finding out who we are during that first half hour at least four times we had to remind ourselves that we really wanted to talk about ourselves. the "straight" women always bring the man into the discussion. i accept this now and see how to deal with it how to expel the man so we can get on with our business. there're always a few standard questions appeals and challenges "i'm made to feel as if i'm not a proper feminist because i'm not a lesbian"—"don't women have the same problems relating to each other as women and men"—"what about *human* liberation"—"why do we have to have these categories, straight and gay, or straight, lesbian, bisexual, etc"—"why can't we be everything or anything when we feel like it." these are a few. fortunately there was a woman at evergreen who took on the categories question eloquently and as "mediator" i seized her reply and tried to elaborate on it and then seized another elaboration by snowshoe until this particular "confrontation" evaporated with an understanding of why we think it's necessary as an expedient at any point in history to call ourselves something. for me the most delicate and dangerous moment arises around what to say to a woman who's still living intimately with a man and finds herself in the midst of a bunch of political women who're threatening her personal solution which she has every right to and who wants to know what you envision for the future and implicitly is asking how to reconcile her present possibly satisfying solution with a feminist ideology which clearly contradicts what she's doing. in this case a beautiful sensitive confused woman bravely exposed herself and her name was cameron and when she asked me whether what we meant was should she exclude men from her life i didn't know what to say i routed around in my head and came up finally with a weak well i guess we're only suggesting that it's something to think about. she was very upset. but she stayed and heard all the stories and at the end she was upset again and a fantastic "connection" appeared, a beaming redhead overalls dyke from around there who wanted to talk to her. make a contact. and i encouraged the connection vigorously before taking off. anyway i saw cameron as a pivotal silent mediator throughout the workshop.

relating connecting conveying transmitting conducting moving bearing relaying implying deploying etc and at the very most producing enormous changes in evolution and at least i've landed in portland i didn't mind relating. again. back. anew. against.

FROM CHAOS WITH LOVE: A TRIBUTE TO SUE

1974-11-07

oct 15 a woman was driving me to the sanfrancisco airport for a 5:23 p.m. flight to st louis. at the twa desk the ticket agent said my plane had left already at 2:30, i guess i might've considered that nothing leaves at 23 after or before the hour. but in my travelling stupor i'd read the ticket wrong by slurring the date and time figures together: 10/15230. actually i'd read the ticket correctly in the sense that 10/1 appeared in the date box and 523 in the time box, with the 0for 230 cut straight down in the middle half in the time box and half in the status box. so i was paying attention to the time and not the date. i mean i *knew* it wasn't october 1st. anyway you don't have to check the date when you know already that the day is correct. this had been determined the day before when i thought i was due in st louis the night of that day and found out through a phone conversation that it was only the 14th. anyway since i missed my flight the following day the 15th i was forced to reflect on the interkarmic reasons for all my mistakes including the misguided computer of the ticket agencies and decided that i had unfinished business in sanfrancisco and that st louis wasn't ready for me yet. i made a reservation for 7 hours later on a 12:45 am flight which would arrive at 6 in time for a morning gig at washington university. the problem of sleep became a high strategic priority. i crashed for 3 hours back in the city, then about 2½ hours on the plane, then 40 minutes in st louis after two women from the u drove me to the "chancellor's house" now a sumptuous southern colonial guest residence. i had no trouble on a luxurious plump purple canopied bed in the master bedroom since i imagined that i was roped off in a museum and nobody could touch me. i woke up fresh as a midwestern buttercake and had a wealthy bath in the kind of bath where a duct in the middle of the tub rushes a reservoir into your own house or tub and causes you to feel like a whirlpool in a therapy. i dressed in my last clean shirt & boots and by this time the two women who'd picked me up had called a lot of the women who were at the reception party dance the night before that i'd missed and they were arriving downstairs to talk about something. there was a lot of anxiety about whether we could stay there and have our coffee and donuts or not since one (black) woman takes care of the "entire mansion" and we would have to "clean up after ourselves." i liked the dining room with its conference size mahogany see-yourself table. we pledged to be good and we stayed. st louis seemed promising. i'd never been there before except to re-enplane for carbondale once and to drive through it on the way to the coast and i had no good reason to expect any plump purple beds or reservoir baths much less the sort of reception that was in store for me. i have an intense eastern chauvinism about the midwest and the father of my children was born and brought up in or around st louis itself and the last weird thing i heard about the place was that masters & johnson do their scientific voyeurism there. nonetheless and/or because of or in spite of these and unforeseen astrological collisions st louis turned out to be like winning the rose bowl. the day itself was a doubleheader. at 2 pm i flew out on delta for charlotte northcarolina and lost heavily there that evening. i won't mention it. since i'm not in training and i don't have a coach or a campaign manager to do strategic reconnaisance i remain completely mystified by the high variation in response from one area to another. i do know one thing i can't hit a homerun in a park that's nearly empty because nobody hardly advertised my arrival. i could barely hit a single in charlotte. but i wasn't going to mention it. all i know for certain now is that i'm very turned on by a huge audience and a high amp system. nor do i apologize for the situation. if you're gonna do it at all you should do it big. if you're busting a gut to enter the midwest or otherwise expose yourself to strangers and the great washed muddle-classes and you're still saying deeply offensive things you should say it to as many people at once as possible in order to get it over with. on a situation like st louis you could almost retire. after talking about things at the chancellor's house over the mahogany table we walked over to the university chapel which is a small cathedral. i waited in a minister's antechamber checking my fast pulse. the organ was revving the place up and you could smell the crowd. the amp system was sensational. the sight of 2000 people or so jammed into a religious structure could give you the illusion that at last you've made your points to the population at large. in this case I owe the illusion in some important measure to sue schneider, to whom my efforts here as another report in progress are a tribute. i wasn't happy to see her there. sue may have the worst reputation of any woman in new york. i *was* happy in a way actually. in the middle of hordes of strangers it's reassuring to see a familiar face and sue is very familiar. also naturally her bad reputation for me is a recommendation. for a while the only new york people who would regularly get in touch with me were the most stigmatized: sue & the holy spirit. as for sue i never would play her alcohol game so i suppose i saw only the best of her and when i did see the worst it was in public circumstances. nonetheless i wasn't overjoyed to see her in st louis. i'd heard she was back on the bottle and she'd left the country near new paltz where she'd been renting something and her animals died there. that was a few months ago. she'd been stone sober for at least a year or so i don't know what happened. i had a desperate call those few months back wanting to camp out at my place with her animals. i said no. i have plenty of animals around where i am including stray dogs & horses along with the birds & beavers.

the main thing was i could tell she wasn't cool. she said the landlord was throwing her out because she was a "lesie" and the neighbors wouldn't let her play with their children. having refused her demand at that point i figured i was on her real bad list too. everybody who's had anything to do with sue must be on her real bad list. as one woman put it she puts herself in a position but what you can't help but let her down. one favor breeds the need for another and another but you don't even have to refuse a request to be her enemy since society is her enemy and we all belong to society and sue is her own worst enemy and so aren't we all when we're down an out. i phoned a few women in new york the other day for feedback on sue or snue as i call her sometimes, wondering partly if it was advisable to write anything about her at all. marcia segerberg told me i decidedly should not but marcia is just as angry as snue in her own way and her negative clauses made me perversely determined to go ahead. one of her objections was that i'd be contributing to the victim image which is sue's prime identity. but since i never participated directly in her victim alcohol game but gave credence instead wherever i saw it (privately) to the contributive and creative sue which is a considerable but underdeveloped self if that makes contradictory sense i decided that if i wrote about her seriously i could only emphasize this side of her that nobody recognizes. i mean recognition in a broader sense than the acknowledgement of these qualities by certain intimates and the concession of them by others, even those she's run through the most. i'm not sure what i mean really, but she is screaming for recognition, i don't know of a public situation where she hasn't demanded attention, and gotten it, and i can't believe she doesn't want to take sober responsibility in the community cause i've seen her do it and i believe in that and besides the things she's known the best for which are her worst she's a farout righton fuckedup frail amazon mutant beautiful sad funny mean down deprived spoiled dizzy derelict dangerous and despairing woman. i don't believe her star has to rise and set over her alcoholism. nor do i believe one has to "earn" private or public recognition, in the conventional sense, anyhow i think she's a pivotal figure in the movement in new york if for no other reason than that she's challenged the feminist & personal & cultural conscience of hundreds of women. the verdict doesn't sound good. marcia said there's nothing you can do about sue, take it from the entire new york community. one of the problems is that people think something *does* have to be "done about" her. then when nothing else can "be done" i suppose with some justification she might be hailed as the first lesbian/feminist martyr of the movement in new york, provided she completes her victim image trip, i was less and less in the mood for the monumental mutual trashing of the woman's scene in new york. if sue had a fault or a virtue it was to throw it all back at everybody with a monumental vengeance. with the help of booze she mirrored in caricature the great & sad spectacle of a movement inverted and lashing at itself like a foaming dragon beating itself to death with its own tail for want of a better victim in the manner characteristic of the socially oppressed when they can't get themselves together personally and/or they feel that their political efforts have been in vain and it's impossible to strike the real oppressor. you have to play it to survive if you're in the middle of it, otherwise you're intolerably agreeable and nobody can tolerate that. sue is theatrically masterful. i was speaking of her in the past tense, but there she was alive & well in st louis, looking pretty healthy too i have to add, without wishing to offend her detractors or doomsayers, and she made her entrance in style (marcia told me style makes a star not what they do) on cue calculated to draw prime attention and i had to admire the timing. a real friendly washington u woman had just introduced me and there's always a splitsecond vacuum created by the exit of the introducer and the command by the speaker, into this vacuum sue arose miraculously from the depths of the audience to appear in front of me on the stage beside the podium and accompanied by a big shaggy grey dog. we embraced ritually before the hushed 2000 and i was really glad. then she joined several women behind me and i forgot about her. i read the piece i'd just written in sanfrancisco, then played infield & outfield or catcher for all the fouls bloopers flies or line drives from the audience. nobody was getting on base. i had a lively largely receptive sympathetic & turned on mess of students and command of this fantastic amp system. however at some point snue became restless and vocal, pacing around the stage hurling "offstage" imprecations into vaulted spaces as well as hassling me personally so i began to feel like i was handling 2000 people with my left hand & snue with my right and i didn't dig it. i was making asides to her with increasing frequency, in t.a. language, white, the aggressor, wins either way (spilling, anal aggression etc): if black shows anger white can feel justified in her resentment, if black restrains herself, white can go on enjoying her opportunities.—i can play white quite well myself so i know the game. in this case i was checked by an "alien" audience and bonding with sue seemed essential so i was trapped between my intrepid impending uproarious "sister" and our common "parent" who must've been perplexed by the relationship. i've never been faced with a situation like this on the road so i had no stock solutions and it was a real dilemma. thus i felt saved by a bell in some remote region of my cortex when at one moment snue happened to be parallel to me several yards distant she caught my eye and i looked over as she was turning away and challenging me over her left shoulder with a hard glare i put out my right arm instinctively and possibly mumbled comere but i don't remember anyway. she responded to the right arm and walked over to the podium where immediately she poured forth some bile into the mike. then i or we was saved by one more bell. it suddenly occurred to me that sue originated in or around st louis and although i've known this very well for some time the knowledge didn't surface in these circumstances till just that second and then it all fell into place, for me at least. i played slick interviewer to a difficult guest. first i said you came from around here didn't you sue and that was all she needed to focus her attention, she launched into her i-was-expelled-from-college-for-being-a-lesbian story, then i got rid of sue after she told her story by asking or telling her if I could say something about her now myself and she walked away right away but looking back at me over that left shoulder. i turned and squared off at the assembly, i said sue was a street fightin dyke from new york and that she'd done a lot of important—i broke off and had my own terrible moment of reckoning which threatened to become public—i had a rush of feeling and choked up—and a woman in the audience helped out … rabble rousing, important rabble rousing, and i claimed my composure. then i told how a couple of years ago sue & me had collaborated spontaneously on an action in new york to disrupt the meetings of the steering committee to organize the annual august woman's march by electing as many dykes as possible to be speakers. sue had credibility with the lower east side dykes and she brought them out to put up their hands and vote for our own. i had more clout for nominating and endorsing them and between us i think we created an inflammatory atmosphere in which we got our dyke speakers over the dead bodies of quite a few "straight" women. there was never another august march. and the media never told why.

TRIBUTE TO SUE (cont'd.)

1974-11-14

i was saying last week in the first of these two parts concerning mostly sue schneider that there was never another august woman's march and the media never told why. this was two years ago. by that time in new york the woman's movement was infested by the bug for a new sexual identity. i could guess there were 10 or 20 conversions a day. however, the new lesbians were another breed from the old lavender menace lesbians angry initially at "gay oppression" and only later at "woman oppression." the new lesbians coming out through feminism enjoyed a consensus reality for their shocking sexuality that every "old dyke" had to forge painfully out of a revolutionary consciousness in collaboration with other besieged women and during a short honeymoon with homosexual males. thus the corny war cry was out of the closet & into the streets. the new wave of lesbians ironically brought their our sexuality back into the closets, many of them being "privileged feminists" who couldn't afford to risk such exposure. millett's embattled position between the two is well known. certain compromises were struck by such articles as ann koedt's getting behind a smokescreen of an "interview" with two women who had come out and whose love for each other was a "special case" or without political significance—a straight feminist line that was abhorrent to the new lesbian/feminist ideological integration. sue was a street fighting lavender menace woman who probably never got over her expulsion from school. i don't know the extent of her activities in the early actions, but i do know she's worked hard on the lesbian switchboard. she's made plenty of trouble besides her own. that at some point it's difficult if not impossible to distinguish private problems from revolutionary issues, that she's played relentlessly on the sympathies of women who have a new compassion for "sisters" as well as on the regular vulnerability of women to the appeal of a helpless child. and that her struggle with alcohol is serious & heroic. after ending up in a coma in a hospital over a year & a half ago she was persuaded to make a heavy protracted effort to get it under control. every few weeks i had a call from her announcing the number of days and i would offer the appropriate congratulations. i imagine she called absolutely everybody for reinforcement. somewhere along there she had a birthday and i couldn't make the party but i sent along a phi beta kappa key. when her scene split apart a few months ago she was on the warpath again. like i said her animals died up in the country where she was renting a cabin or something. i had this desperate call i didn't respond to and the only thing i heard before i saw her in st louis oct 16 was how she created a little havoc at ms magazine. i was told she went up there wanting to see gloria and a place to stay. she went up three days in a row. the first time she was "definitely drunk" and they gave her some money to eat. the second time she "could hardly stand up" and she wanted money to buy a dog because she said her dog had died. one of those days gloria was touched by sue's sad story about her grandmother back home around st louis who was old but lively and about to be "put away" by "the family" and gloria sent her a dozen roses which was a mistake from the point of view that it would encourage sue to go for more and put you in the guilty sadistic position of letting her down by throwing her out. one favor breeds the need for another and another but you don't have to refuse a request to be her enemy since at least when she's drunk everybody is her enemy before she arrives even. i know for myself if i sent roses to her grandmother i'd feel certain that the next thing i'd have to do would be to send her carrots to her horse and bones to her dog and take sue herself on a magical mystery tour to the amazon basin where the fabulous nations of maidens on mounted demons are galloping from the edges of the world to make ice and golden sand splash to all sides, or something. something anyway infinitely and endlessly satisfying. the world as a sour mash tennessee nipple. FU i loved the high cloud and the hill, alas, he died of alcohol. sue already died of alcohol. i think this last binge is a mere memory trip. anyway she didn't look bad at all in st louis as i mentioned and she was travelling with a shaggy grey dog and a woman called susan who was probably her last rescuer. the way berne defines it in games people play "alcohol" is a four-handed game for which all parties obtain primary and secondary gains. there's a rescuer, a persecutor, a dummy, and one who is "it." the persecutor might be a spouse and the rescuer a physician and the dummy a more or less indifferent person who simply offers supplies when needed and may also act as a passive object for instinctual impulses, usually both libidinal and aggressive. the roles can be condensed into a three-handed or two-handed game and can also be switched. according to berne rescue organizations like aa offer the best chance for cessation of drinking because they provide all the roles in a reliable continuity, as a private person i'm a confused "dummy" myself. i wouldn't send roses but i have offered supplies, namely my hospitality when the victim was sober. also told i the story of collaborating with sue two years ago on that action in new york to disrupt the meetings of the steering committee organizing the annual august woman's march by electing as many dykes as possible to be our speakers. sober i'd trust her in a revolutionary cadre to save the world. she's fearless and steadfast. she's a woman accustomed to death. and she probably wouldn't be anything if you paid her, she has the highest credentials as a welfare dyke. recently i had a letter from a lavender menace woman, an artist who retreated to her work and her lover, and she wrote me that in those days she was "caught up in the mass hysteria of hatred for anyone who did anything," that when she lived in chinatown and i used to come and visit she was always too much in awe of who i was to see me as flesh and blood, to her i was a massive ego who freaked her out cause at that time she didn't know how to react to the woman who was supposed to be a "star." i'm looking for a recent letter from marci who said something to the effect how i'd like to make sue into my own crappy stinking star image. but sue already is a star. she has the worst reputation of any woman in new york. a nice dyke at this time in history is a contradiction in terms and sue may be the angriest of us all. i heard she bombarded the mike at the christopher street gay liberation march this july wearing all black and brandishing bunches of black balloons and belting out amazon alcoholic fury. sue's a heavy balloon person. once when she was nice & creative & sober she climbed my hill and took it as if it were a bunker i guess and planted some white ones up at the top someplace written in red or blood dyke nation or lesbiansignite or sappho was a righton lavender balloon. she really is a poet and she draws the finest pictures too. she may not belong to the welfare crowd at all. she's a thinking dreaming reading writing talking drawing & painting person. as marcia said why don't you (me) write about somebody who's *doing* something. that would mean somebody who's opening a woman's coffeehouse or restaurant and painting houses not pictures and learning how to fix yer own wheels or thdkench to sdcytrchktovb & siehn downt, dnaekchemd ksiehdnjsklmfhens sicheil. anyway i identify with snue. i see me in her in me her me. meeting everybody grownup not knowing who we all were. she was allergic to her own body bacteria. first i noticed her boots were unpolished. next i noticed she misspelled a whole lot of words. next i noticed she takes real big steps & i couldn't keep up with her. then she talks loud even when or especially when no-one is listening. she had a setback when her hair dangled in the cafeteria food, they accused her of it. etc. going back a step i would ask, in the alcohol game, what are those primary and secondary gains that all parties who play it obtain. since i'm into the berne-harris ta terminology i'll pursue the thought according to that line. many people still wish to play the parent okay role to any not-okay child. harris defines our original position in life as the not-okay (helpless, dependent) child in relation to the okay parent. i'm not okay, you're okay. the classic cultural male-female positioning is i'm okay (male). you're not okay (female). in turn the woman is okay to her not-okay children who sometimes grow up to be okay and get off on other people not being okay or more unusually like other people to be okay too and that's the title of harris's bestseller: i'm okay-you're okay. when a friend of yours is down whatdyou do, do you withdraw, do you try to talk them out of it, are you solicitous, do you use them for your own battleground, giving advice or arguing as if they were your own problems, dyou feel better or more powerful when somebody else is down, etc. here's a harris quote that sums up the parent-child situation. "the person whose not-okay Child is always activated cannot get on with transactions which will advance his dealing with reality because he is continually concerned with unfinished business having to do with a past reality. he can't accept a compliment gracefully because he doesn't think he deserves it, and there must be a barb in it somewhere. he is involved in a continuous attempt to maintain the integrity of the position that was established in the situation of childhood. the person who always comes on Child is really saying 'look at me, i'm not okay.' the person who is always coming on Parent is really saying, 'look at you, you're not okay (*and that makes me feel better*).' both maneuvers are an expression of the not okay position and each contributes to the prolongation of despair." (gender harris's, lowercase & italics mines). the okay position of the parent is a putup job. no parent can be okay when half the planet is down because they're up. the way i see it in woman terms all the women i know are wondering how they can be okay when they grew up under the heavy injunction that they'd better not be okay when their mothers couldn't be okay. the mother-daughter position culturally is i'm not okay-you're not okay. when the mother & daughter commiserate they're having a complementary parent-parent or child-child transaction, both being not okay. when the mother is urging her daughter through her own acculturated mode to become another oppressed mother she's substantiating the mutual not-okay position. when the mother objects to her daughter's independent moves and the daughter fights back the transaction is crossed parent-child. anyway snue has been stuck in the not-okay position, "continually concerned with unfinished business having to do with a past reality." when she was sober she couldn't stop talking about alcohol and how she wasn't doing it anymore and nobody should (she was taking up the attitude of the rescuer) and she never could stop raving about being a dyke and how every woman is or should be. i don't know how any one person begins to feel more relaxed and confident about a novel revolutionary identity but i do know that many women do and they're now getting on with the total business of living of playing & working with the base of a new assured political sexual identity. a serious problem is one whole strata of the movement in new york has been the conflict between asserting oneself and doing things and the fear that one's activities would incur public notice and snue as i said is a thinking dreaming reading writing talking drawing & painting type of person which is a type that tends to draw public attention so the "good" parent in me believes that snue would be better off being herself without the censorship of her welfare peers who themselves may be happier in their ideological anonymous purity. anyhow one continually sees situations begetting their own opposites. the woman who hates stars today is a star tomorrow. another likeable culture villain joins the ranks. everyone here is a revolutionary. they all sit around eating yogurt. if we become too serious we lose our way.

and there is so much to do so much to say, a woman at a gig in new york last week said what can we do and i said we're doing it right now. in st louis there was a critical revolutionary moment at the end when i was going to the airport and snue wanted to go with me and i didn't want her to. i asked her friend susan to tell her for me and susan said i should really tell her myself, that snue would understand if i was straight with her. so i did and it was okay. i said listen snue i'm all revved up and i have to rev down and i want to go to the airport alone, she accepted that silently, we embraced again, and that's the revolution, a direct stimulus & an appropriate response. i may disagree with the whole new york community but i think snue has come a long way. the first time i saw her she was drooling & staggering & being held up by two other women. the second time i saw her she looked like her face had been hit by a mack truck. every many times i saw her she was making a public exhibition of herself as the prime victim of the universe. but i've seen by this time a lot of her healthy constructive sides too and her trip to help her grandmother is a trip to save herself as well. so i say fuck all her doomsayers and from chaos with love to sue schneider: a brave crazy essential woman of the new york movement. (caution: this life can be hazardous to your life).

Part 2

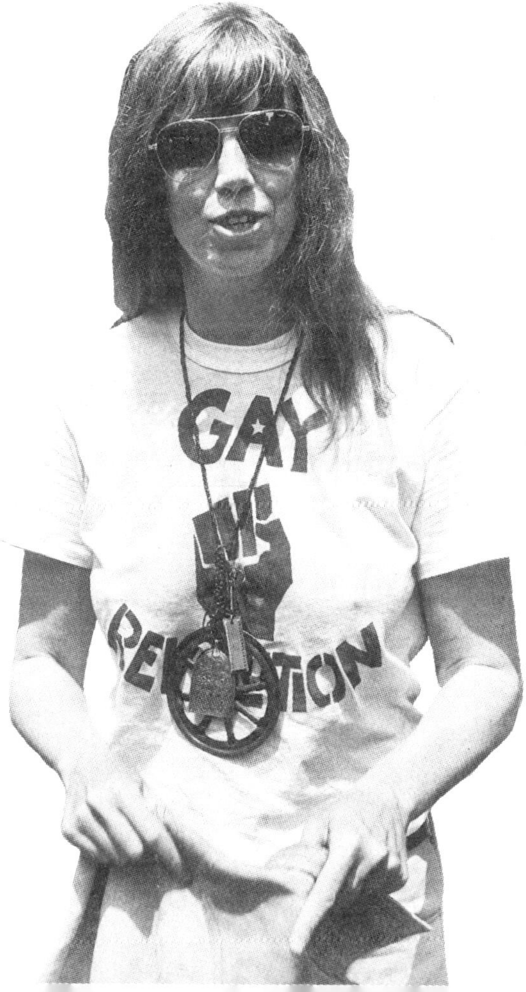

Reflections

WRITE FIRST THEN LIVE[1]

Ingrid Nyeboe

It was the mid-1960s, I had finished college, started PhD courses in Theater History/Dramaturgy at the University of Copenhagen (Denmark), and had begun what would turn out to become a habit: traveling as often and for as long as possible in Europe, including some of the then behind-the-iron-curtain countries. I always had a good justification: looking at theater, doing research on playwrights, productions, design etc.

On one such trip, I came across a copy of *The Village Voice*. My recall is that I was in Amsterdam—and read the newspaper from cover to cover. What caught my attention more than anything else was the "Dance Journal" by Jill Johnston; unfortunately I can't pinpoint the exact column. Suffice it to say, I was hooked and upon my return to Copenhagen I got a subscription to the VV and became, just like hundreds of other people, addicted to her writing. It was like a mammoth spring-cleaning, windows were opened not just to let in fresh air. Windows I never even knew existed opened up to make me view unexpected unanticipated brand new unusual vistas as well as challenging me to different ways of seeing.

Four years after my initial encounter with Jill's writing, I arrived in New York and figured out a way to stay, partly so I could station myself each Tuesday evening near the office of *The Village Voice* to pick up my weekly fix of her writing—on everything new, outrageous, avant-garde, and generally shocking.

She is an erudite artist incarnate
a writer who,
like a choreographer/dancer,
understands everything about the unending permutations of the body in motion, in time, in space
……. and writes like that
a writer who,
like a composer,
structures every piece in infinite ways, sees the hues of the notes, and creates sounds and silences
……. and writes like that
a writer who,
like a critic,
has a comprehensive knowledge, a profound respect and compassion for her subject and gives us new ways of comprehending
……. and writes like that
a writer who,
like a painter,
relishes in colors, hues, drips, mark making, strokes, negative space, the rectangle so identical to the white page
……. and writes like that
a writer who,
like a poet,
savors each word, each syllable, each letter
……. and writes like that

a writer who,
like a sculptor,
chisels cuts molds wrestles out of bronze, marble, steel, stone, wood
.... and writes like that
a writer who, intuitively and intellectually, rolled all her exquisite and varied abilities, her renaissance-like knowledge into the service of her craft. And we are the fortunate ones, enriched by her writing.

At the end of the day, she is the woman with whom I spent four plus decades, three of those in a loving, intimate and inspiring relationship, the woman I love and honor in big and small ways, the woman who got up each morning to do the utterly mundane things living well requires of us.

1 I've borrowed the title to this piece from the original title to "Fictions of the Self in the Making" by Jill Johnston, published in the *New York Times Book Review* on April 25, 1993.

P.S. A special thank you to Megan and Fiona for their insistence on guiding me through what is a difficult, delicate and exciting process: sharing my beloved Jill, her spirit and her work. Thank you to Axel and every person associated with the exhibition at Bergen Kunsthall, Bergen, Norway.

Bruce Hainley

dear megan,

i just watched *april 30, 1971, new york* for the first time—often referred to as *town bloody hall*, after something germaine greer says during the proceedings: ostensibly intellectual theater, a debate on feminism, the thing's quickly hijacked (courtesy of bulldozing moderator norman mailer), retooled to an actuarial in mansplaining, before the term existed but obviously not before the thing itself. jill's there, amused, bemused, the muse, working her long hair and tinted aviator glasses, snug in her jean jacket with union jack and flower appliqués, seated next to diana trilling the entire time, until she (jj) gets up to speak, speaks, and, just reaching cruising speed, is cut short by mailer. most of the audience—captivated, loving every joke and pun, her fun, her sinuous sentences snaking around a quotation, letting it go—cheers for her to continue. after she's been cut short, two women climb up on stage and she makes out with them; they roll around on the floor, kissing. bored with mansplaining. a de-mailer but not really a de-maler, jj leaves with one of her make-out partners, stage right.

she knew how to exit, and how to enter. her first two sentences in "new approach," her "episode" for *town hall*: "all women are lesbians—except those who don't know it naturally. they are but don't know it yet." she keeps punning on the "naturally," as anyone naturally alive to language naturally would. *april 30, 1971, new york* is a strange document. from the footage available, i'm not sure there's any surprise or point—it's difficult to see the big or bigger picture in any fervent moment (just think how barbaric we'll seem to people 50 years from now, if civilization survives)—in noting that no one black seems to be at town hall, a fact quietly emphasized when susan sontag, special guest, comments that no woman wants to be referred to as the "foremost lady critic" (mailer's designation of diana trilling) any more than james baldwin would want to be called the foremost negro writer; not on stage, not in the audience, no black person in the entire bloody hall, perhaps, until, near the very end, anatole aroyard asks a question, and at that point black's not how he was presenting himself. to nutshell his complicated appearance (does "passing" cover it?) is beyond my ken, and jj's long gone by his question anyway. she wins the crowd, makes out, and leaves—off to cooler scenes, a lesbian lenny bruce. she liked to have her cock and eat it too, she'd quipped.

right now, i'm listening to ariana grande and paging back and forth through the little portfolio of black-and-white photos that appear about two-thirds of the way through *gullibles travels* (new york: links books, 1974). i'd intended to write new captions for many of them, and even for some that don't exist, but the fact of these pictures overwhelms me, their tenderness and frivolity, their communal eroticism. more than a few of them are credited to roz gerstein (all lowercase letters in the original), who created *the original women's yellow pages sourcebook*, a bestseller, which had editions in many parts of northeastern america. about the first photographic project she lists on her website (www.rozgerstein.com), she writes: "in 1975 i photographed and interviewed a small community of runaways, addicts, pimps, and prostitutes who gathered daily on the boston common seeking fellowship and support—misery looking for company. i remain friends with ricky, one of the original subjects." a picture by roz gerstein opens the *gullibles travels* album: "jj in motion." our subject centers or decenters the frame, a blur, all energy and spirit. jj's captioned the photo: "*i imagine i'm being pursued by an amazon posse*." some of the posse poses in the pictures that follow, wearing stovepipes and porkpies and cowboy hats, often eschewing patronyms: rena, jane, alison, sara, lin, meg, maureen, all photographed by carol dear, the book's designer. poised and regal, rena patterson and dianna hunter, both by linda kieves. agnes martin. sk dunn looking like a matinee idol (jj comments: "*heroic nudity would also be more appropriate on this occasion*.") amelia earhart (courtesy of *the women's yellow pages*). pauline oliveros riding an elephant in mid-curtsy (a marvel, credited to becky cohen). jj's daughter winnie and son richard, her "*amazon children*." i'd like to say the final man is a queen (the great gregory battcock, writer, editor, bon vivant, luxury ocean liner aficionado—he poses in his state room aboard the *mikhail lermontov,* an open bottle of tattinger in front of him), but that's not how the pictures are sequenced. some of the women are called by nicknames or protective aliases: "snowshoe" and "strawberry." *all women are lesbians—except those who don't know it naturally.* other pix by roz gerstein take pride of place: on the front cover, jj, legs crossed, seated on a wooden chair, a big manual typewriter on the ground to the left of her, sports a derby hat, a military jacket, jeans, and boots, for a pic i'd caption, *jj having just invented steampunk*; and on the back, she walks alone down a dirt road in autumn, her back to the camera.

probably my favorite way to watch her is in andy warhol's *jill and freddy dancing*, 1963. jj cavorts on a rooftop with fred herko. they're both so beautiful, and they look to be having so much fun, and watching them, knowing that andy's camera's trained on them, how could anyone ever think he was asexual? it's not not a *pas de deux*, and, given andy's palpable extradiegetic glee, it's also not not a *pas de trois*. there are many ways to dance. he filmed gay and lesbian joy, among other things, them dancing, and it's something too rare in the world or on film. she caught so much of it in writing.

because it's been on my own mind a lot, ways of writing, genres, i've been wondering why jj never wrote a novel. not that i know or care what a novel is. what's collected in *gullibles travels* she calls "*writing*"—not essays, not fiction, not memoir. the photo suite, hell, just the pictures of pauline oliveros, enlisting the elephant in her campaign for new sounds and new ways of being, as well as sk dunn, hunk, make up (*pace* Roland Barthes) *la préparation du roman*. perhaps the preparation of the novel is better than any novel. my single favorite work by jj, "agnes martin: surrender & solitude," closes *gullibles travels*. it's a picaresque tale but also a kind of pilgrim's progress, the femme trekking across country to the butch, trying to make sense of her taciturnity and abstention. its last six sentences read: "in albuquerque after she drove us out and we were having brunch in la placita i asked her if she didn't think she was leading an exemplary life and once again she knocked the whole thing, oh my no, i'm a murderer, i'm a this and a that, i'm working out the hairy ape in myself, i'm just beginning, and so on, and i remembered how she leaned forward intensely in the adobe and said somewhat incredulously and you realized how mean we all are and i nodded yes, so how could i exempt her from her own conclusions about life. the work is the thing. the grid is still because the whole can be grasped by the eye and mind at once. the value she places on the known rather than the seen suggests innate ideas which she sometimes calls a memory of perfection. agnes martin: a study in the memories of perfection. "the ocean is deathless/ the islands rise and die/ quietly come, quietly go/ a silent swaying breath/ i wish the idea of time would drain/ out of my cells and leave me/ quiet even on this shore."

at a not minor moment in the cultural history of new york, she was alive to everyone and everything and channeled that ebb and flow into writing. we haven't really come to grips with what jj did, no labanotation for her madcap, bittersweet choreography, her life, except, of course, her words.

fondly,

JILL JOHNSTON: THE I OF THE BEHOLDER

Jennifer Krasinski

"Enthusiasm is not the same as falling in love," Jill Johnston reflected in 1979.[1] If enthusiasm glosses, overlooks, then love apprehends dimensions, contradictions. Love sees clearly. Johnston became a critic because she fell in love with dance. With no previous professional writing experience, she published her first piece in 1955, an essay titled "Thoughts on the Present and Future Directions of Modern Dance," in *Dance Observer*, a journal founded by choreographer, composer and critic Louis Horst.[2] (Johnston would one day tip her hat to Horst as a model critic for his review of "7 New Dances" by Paul Taylor, who was then exploring the merits

1 Jill Johnston, "How I Became an Art Critic and How I Do It Now," *The Village Voice*, November 5, 1979, 40.
2 Jill Johnston, "Thoughts on the Present and Future Directions of Modern Dance," *Dance Observer*, no. 22 (August–September 1955), 101–102.

of minimalism. Horst cheekily commemorated the program's relative lack of movement by publishing two inches of blank space.) Two years later, Johnston began writing and reviewing for the paper with greater regularity, covering Taylor, James Waring, as well as offering up think pieces like "The Modern Dance—Directions and Criticisms," and "Abstraction in Dance," both from 1957.

Her earliest ink spills form a portrait of a young critic who's finding her feet, freshly tapping into the cracks and crevices of her own brain, developing her ideas, her voice, her moves. She more or less adheres to the form, dutifully leading with the what, when and where of the performances, punctuating most of her reviews by listing the dancers, or giving a one-sentence acknowledgement to a member of the creative team, or ticking off certain other boxes on a typical critic's clunky to-do list. Yet her wit, her vim, ribbed decorum even then, and she always wrote her own mind about what she saw. She herself would cover a performance by Taylor and Company on December 20, 1958, stepping in where Horst's silence had left off: "They attempt stillness in extreme, about as far as could be managed without doing nothing—a few changes of position, a little walking around. *Epic* requires a greater projection of presence than Mr. Taylor can now muster..."[3]

Perhaps because Waring received more favorable reviews from Johnston—"a brawling Joke, not without its finesse, in keeping with an outlook that is tired of logical continuities and doesn't mind telling you so in so many motions"[4]—he recommended her for the position of dance critic at New York's iconoclastic weekly paper, *The Village Voice*, which was, in Johnston's words, "a 13 page rag at the time." As America's first alternative weekly, the *Voice* was an oasis for the vociferous and the unbending, muckrakers and rebels,

3 *Dance Observer*, vol. 26, no. 2 (February 1959), 25.
4 *Dance Observer*, vol. 26, no. 5 (May 1959), 74.

upstarts and eccentrics, and unafraid to give column inches to radical politics, difficult ideas and unpopular opinions.

The paper proved to be an ideal springboard for Johnston, encouraging (or at least not impeding) her fullest expression as a writer and thinker, giving her free rein to cover both what compelled her, and what repelled her. Her column debuted on February 3, 1960, and would remain hers until 1967. Some months after she started working at the *Voice*, her beat unexpectedly expanded when she penned a letter to the editor of *Art News*, defending Abstract Expressionism from the nasty lash of John Canaday, then the conservative, contentious art critic for the *New York Times*. The editor responded to Johnston's corrective by inviting her to write reviews for the magazine. With only two art history classes and a single course in studio art under her belt, she accepted the offer. Years later, she would quip: "In a hated profession, I had an excellent start."[5]

In the early '60s, Johnston's prose grew longer legs, becoming more agile and perambulatory. As a writer, and as an audience member, Johnston had tremendous presence and range. Her reviews—penned in an immersive present-tenseness, and written with increasing frequency in the first person—punctured the myth of the passive audience. Rather, she proved that audience *is* action, is a mode of production, of meaning, as she matched the momentum of downtown New York's wildly escalating art and performance scenes, which were hell-bent on collapsing genres, concocting hybrid forms, and injecting lightness and delight into the rigors of artistic practice. Pop, via Andy Warhol, Claes Oldenburg and others, was dissolving the distinctions between high and low culture, between audience and consumer. Happenings were happening via the likes of Allan Kaprow and others who stoked the present moment so that it burned intensely for both participants and attendees alike. "So now we are speaking of theater (art) in general, or life in general," Johnston wrote

5 "How I Became an Art Critic and How I Do It Now," 39.

of the newfangled category in 1962. "Where one begins and the other ends is one of the interesting questions..."[6]

In the summer of that same year, a group of budding young choreographers presented a selection of new works at the Judson Memorial Church. Titled simply "A Concert of Dance," the evening would be a watershed moment, announcing the arrival of a new vanguard, and soon catapulting Lucinda Childs, Simone Forti, David Gordon, Deborah Hay, Freddie Herko, Yvonne Rainer, Carolee Schneemann, Steve Paxton and more into dance history. Johnston was one of the first to anoint them, individually and collectively, and would thereafter consistently review performances by the community referred to as the Judson Dance Theater. She was, in essence, their writer of record; like her subjects, Johnston's typewriter sounded the beat of a different drummer, as it pounded out some of the most evocative documents of that era's live arts. On Steve Paxton's "Afternoon (A Forest Concert)" (1963), which he staged in the woods near the New Jersey home of engineer Billy Klüver, Johnston recalled some of the sum total of a performance pointedly offered outside of a theater space:

> I wasn't keen about the dancing because the ground made balancing difficult and the forest was more exciting than human technique. But I liked the unexpected entrances, the nonchalant disappearances, and not knowing or caring too much where to look when something was going on in a specified vicinity and one or two other things were going on in more distant places.[7]

Writing on "Trio A" of 1964, she explains in language both direct and clear, the nature of Rainer's radical offerings:

6 Jill Johnston, *Marmalade Me* (New York: E. P. Dutton & Co., 1971), 51.
7 *Marmalade Me*, 71.

> *Trio A* was the first fully realized expression of a new position. The shift is most emphatically toward neutrality: toward the matter-of-fact "doing" of a thing rather that the "performing" of a thing, toward a "work-like rather than an exhibition-like presentation," toward a removal of seductive involvement with an audience.[8]

Johnston had by then earned a devoted readership, not least among her peers. She was a star on the scene in her own right, even starring in two Andy Warhol films, *Jill and Freddie Dancing* (1963), for which she pranced and whirled on a Manhattan rooftop alongside dancer and choreographer Freddie Herko, and *Jill Johnston Dancing* (1964), in which she performed a goofball duet with a broom.[9] She was also by then a mother of two, in an unhappy marriage, and finding herself feeling pulled between the obligations prescribed for her by her personal and professional status, and the free-for-all spirit of the age.

* * *

On September 16, 1965, *The Village Voice* published what is now considered one of Johnston's landmark texts, an essay-cum-manifesto titled "Critics' Critics," which she lobbed like a grenade at the producers and consumers of the downtown scene. She had become dispirited that artists responded solely to her opinions, but never to the artfulness of her prose, or the quality of her ideas. Her standing as a critic inside the democratizing spirit of the Judson Dance Theater was a slippery one: She was at once in that world—a participant, a collaborator at times—but her role also set her apart from that world. If critics can admit the call and response nature of art—can allow for the fact that meaning is made between a maker, her work and her audience—then why can't artists do the same?

8 *Marmalade Me*, 39.
9 See *Judson Dance Theater: The Work Is Never Done*, ed. Ana Janevski and Thomas J. Lax (New York: The Museum of Modern Art, 2018), 152.

Weighing on her too was the unsettled, and unsettling matter of authority, which she did not feel she possessed, and yet possess she did, as per her position at the *Voice*.[10] In "Critics' Critics," she carved a new place for herself from which to speak, asserting a prerogative as a creator in her own right:

> Criticism wears me out—it's like riding a bike up and down the country hills in a race against a phantom judge. I'll take a plot of level territory and stake out a claim to lie down on it and criticize the constellations if that's what I happen to be looking at. I also stake out a claim to be an artist, a writer, if that's what I'm doing when I get to the typewriter and decide that I liked something well enough to say what I think it's all about.[11]

If that's what I'm doing. Even inside her declaration, Johnston left room for doubt, for criticism of her criticism, for second-guessing, for dissent. Johnston would later reveal, with her usual candor, that she'd filed "Critics' Critics" while being treated for chronic undifferentiated schizophrenia on the psychiatric ward of Bellevue hospital.[12] In her preface to *Marmalade Me* (1971), a collection of her critical writing from 1960 to 1970, Johnston reflected on her experiences during that era:

> I became what Timothy Leary has called a revelatory casualty and all seemed lost. What had happened seemed very unclear actually except that I had a new career opened up to me as a "mental case" and eventually I decided to exploit it instead of burying it because I had become privately convinced that the society which had stigmatized me as crazy was itself crazy and that through the

10 Jill Johnston, *Paper Daughter. Autobiography in Search of a Father, Vol. 2* (New York: Alfred P. Knopf, 1985), 8.
11 *Marmalade Me*, 100.
12 *Paper Daughter*, 58.

> purgatorial fires of a mind-exploding experience I had, without warning or preparation, become a rather healthy person.[13]

Johnston, by *unbecoming* a critic, was becoming someone and something else. She was, in a sense, writing herself anew.

* * *

In the 1970s, lesbian feminist scholar Karla Jay interviewed Johnston, recording their conversation on a cassette tape, which is now accessible as part of Jay's archives at the New York Public Library.[14] The sound quality of the tape is terrible; as a document, it is all but useless. The women's voices are almost completely drowned out by the ambient noises of what I presume to be the café or restaurant they were sitting in, so that listening to them, even with the volume turned up on a set of headphones, feels more like eavesdropping from two tables away. Only a few phrases ring clearly over the din of chatter and traffic, the clang of dishes and silverware. Johnston's salvageable sound bites—while not as enigmatic or poetic as Sappho's fragments—manage to loosen a few vivid threads from her stories. One in particular could spin reams of writing around her:

> You know, I play the fool a lot.

Johnston spoke these words in a faint, plaintive voice, though it is difficult to discern if her tone is tinted with resignation, or regret, or both, or neither. As a public figure, she had won (and lost) many admirers because of certain of her antics, because of her refusal to behave simply for behavior's sake. Her capers could be disruptive, disrespectful, though largely in keeping with the zeitgeist, or so it seems in hindsight.

13 *Marmalade Me*, 14.

14 Karla Jay Papers 1961–2013 [bulk 1975–1999] MssCol 1554 (New York Public Library, Manuscripts and Archives Division, 03398).

In dramatic literature, of course, the fool is at once comic relief, and as well the character who speaks truth to power, who in the end reveals the foolish structures, the poisonous complicities, that hold power aloft. It is a role that reminds the audience that biting the hand that feeds you, rather than rebelling outright, means your knees are still bent, your mouth open and at the ready.

From 1965 onward, Johnston strayed farther and farther from straight criticism, using her *Voice* column instead to print diaristic accounts of her life and how she lived it. (Another critic, Deborah Jowitt, was hired by the paper in 1967, not to replace her but to cover dance in her stead.)[15] As the fool, Johnston played the part with great gusto and flawless timing. Her entrances were often splashy, as was in fact the case when she got undressed and jumped into the swimming pool during a fundraiser at the chichi home of art collectors Robert and Ethel Scull. ("Well you see I have this resportsibility to make my life interesting to my readers each week," she wrote in her column titled "Bash in the Sculls.")[16] Her arrivals could be just as dramatic. In May of 1969, to celebrate her break from criticism, Johnston invited Warhol, his superstar Ultra Violet, artist Carolee Schneemann, and critics Gregory Battcock and David Bourdon to participate in a panel discussion titled "The Disintegration of a Critic: An Analysis of Jill Johnston." Three hundred people gathered for the art star-studded event, to which Johnston showed up forty minutes late, and then read a text she'd written as her *Voice* column for the following week. For some, her diva turn was a smash. For others, a bomb. A journalist covering the event for *Variety* reported that her performance "confirmed the suspicion that she is as confusing in person as she is in print."[17]

15 https://www.artforum.com/print/201807/deborah-jowitt-76347
16 Jill Johnston, *Admission Accomplished: The Lesbian Nation Years 1970–75* (London: Serpent's Tail, 1998), 10.
17 *Variety*, May 28, 1969, 23.

But it was Johnston's exits that were perhaps her most glorious. She made her first of note in 1969, when she came out in print as a lesbian, becoming one of America's first openly gay journalists. (In a command performance, she would come out again four years later, this time on the popular late-night television talk show, *The Dick Cavett Show*, wearing a great goofy grin and mugging a "Hi Mom!" for the camera.)[18] Her writing freed itself too, becoming what Johnston giddily referred to as "ideal cunnilinguistics," connoting the entwining of speech and desire—text as turn-on.[19] If women's words have traditionally been thought of as gossip, Johnston elevated female *tongue wagging* to something tender, muscular, ravenous, and offered for the express purpose of giving pleasure to women. Her prose rushed like a river after a torrential rainfall, uninterrupted by the strictures of punctuation and capital letters and so forth. Her mission, in her words, was "to mongrelize the language, deform and debase every convention, create a freak of culture, engender a misbegotten blot on the authorial landscape."[20] (Shining examples from this period of her writing would later be collected in *Gullibles Travels* [1974]).

As the fool, she very nearly outdid herself in April of 1971, with a public display so brazen that writer Norman Mailer, himself no stranger to brash, irreverent behavior, allegedly recalled it as "the night that Jill Johnston turned my hair gray."[21] The occasion for Johnston and Mailer's paths crossing was a panel discussion on women's liberation, for which they were joined by literary critic Diana Trilling; president of the National Organization of Woman, Jacqueline Ceballos; and feminist author, Germaine Greer. (The occasion would be memorialized in the documentary *Town Bloody Hall* [1971] by filmmakers D.A. Pennebaker and Chris Hegedus).

18 See Michael Bronski, *Culture Clash: The Making of Gay Sensibility* (Boston: South End Press, 1984), 5.

19 Jill Johnston, *Gullibles Travels* (New York: Links Books, 1974), xi.

20 *Admission Accomplished*, v.

21 *Cineaste*, vol. 41, no. 3 (Summer 2016), 30.

Presented at New York University, the event was packed to the rafters; Betty Friedan and Susan Sontag were just two of the cognoscente in attendance. Moderated by Mailer, the panel would allow for each woman to deliver a brief statement before the conversation began.

When it was Johnston's turn to speak, she took the podium and gave the night's most rousing speech. "Until all women are lesbians, there will be no true political revolution," she declared, words that became the molten core of her groundbreaking collection of essays titled *Lesbian Nation: The Feminist Solution* (1973). Mailer tried to cut her off in the middle of her speech, but she blasted through long enough to proudly proclaim, "this is the body that Jill built"—an expression of radical self-possession. Not to be bested by Mailer's machismo, Johnston, before she left the stage, was joined by two women from the audience, and together they enjoyed a mock threesome, rolling around together on the floor to the shock of some audience members, and to the delight of others.

Johnston would continue to be a regular columnist for the *Voice* until 1975, and she would be celebrated by colleagues such as Jasper Johns, James Lee Byars, Lucas Samaras, Barbara Rose, Meredith Monk, Yvonne Rainer and others in a special issue of the riotous tabloid *Culture Hero*: *A Fanzine of Stars of the Super World*, published by Les Levine in 1970.[22] (One choice bit of praise, reportedly said to Lil Picard by the King of Pop, Warhol himself: "She is very sexy and easy to read. She writes like a Film."[23]) In subsequent years, she sleuthed the unknown source of herself—her father—writing two books, *Mother Bound. Autobiography in Search of a Father, Vol. 1* (1983) and *Paper Daughter. Autobiography in Search of a Father, Vol. 2* (1985). She eventually returned to art and performance criticism in the 1980s, this time for *Art in*

22 See Les Levine, *Culture Hero Masterprint: Jill Johnston Exposed* (New York: N.I.L.), 1970.
23 Ibid, 11.

America. Johnston and her extraordinary writing—documents of an era, records of an exemplary mind—prove that the art and life divide is not only impossible, it is unthinkable. That is, if you believe her words. What is fact if not simply the most convincing fiction? Or as she playfully wrote about her work: "I don't have an interesting life at all. I make it all up."[24]

24 *Marmalade Me*, 208.

Part 3

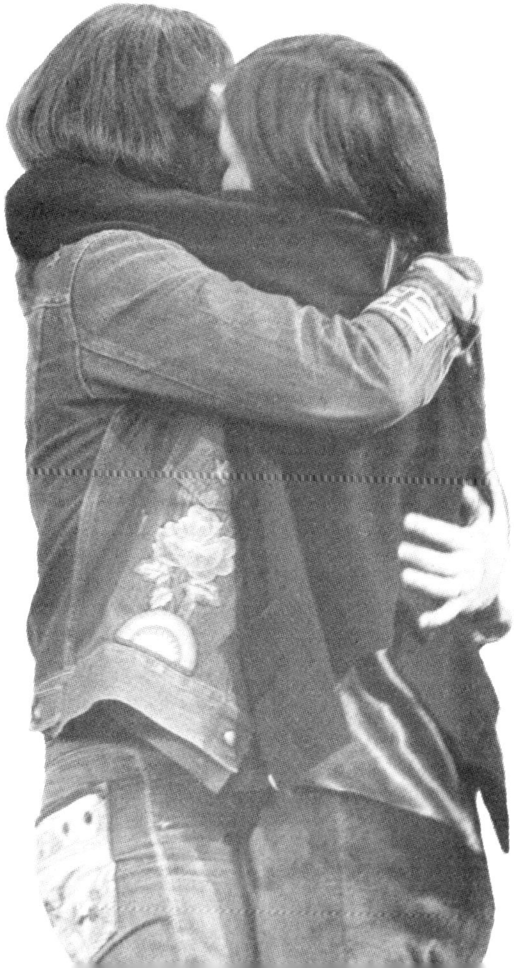

Appendix

at Thomas Hoving might hairman of the National n the Arts, a page one Ted and Ethel Kennedy with their kids, a nn photograph of the Wales, a story about three-column portait of izabeth, a story about admitting coeds in the y about a man lost in a ccident in Long Island two-column picture of Julie Eisenhower going me, another story about e of Wales, a hospital South Carolina, a story ike in California that is from melting snow, a he Cornell siege, a story se Kennedy, one about nt over a Viking map, a Kilmer story, a James ory, and a story about ish schools in Newark, ers.

the fighting in the Ireland doesn't mean

Five: Will somebody please tell me what the hell Jill Johnston is trying to say?

On Miss Johnston

A panel discussion moderated by David Bourdon on "The Disintegration of a Critic: an Analysis of Jill Johnston" will be conducted on Wednesday, May 21, at 8.30 p. m. at NYU's Eisner and Lubin Auditorium, Loeb Student Center, 566 LaGuardia Place. Participants will be psychiatrist Dr. John Atchley; Walter Gutman, securities analyst, artist, writer, film-maker, sugardaddy; art patron John de Menil; film-maker and Kinetic Theatre founder Carolee Schneemann; artist-writer Lil Picard; Andy Warhol; and superstar Ultra Violet. Admission is free.

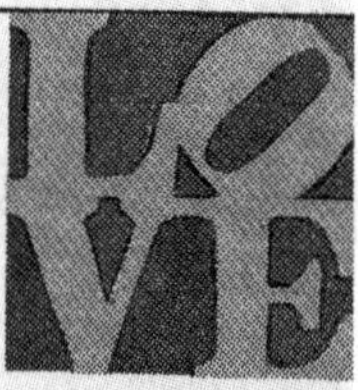

Announcement from *The Village Voice*, April 24, 1969 for the panel discussion "The Disintegration of a Critic: An Analysis of Jill Johnston" at New York University, Loeb Student Center

ON MISS JOHNSTON

A panel discussion moderated by David Bourdon on "The Disintegration of a Critic: an Analysis of Jill Johnston" will be conducted on Wednesday, May 21, at 8.30 p. m. at NYU's Eisner and Lubin Auditorium, Loeb Student Center, 566 LaGuardia Place. Participants will be psychiatrist Dr. John Atchley; Walter Gutman, securities analyst, art, writer, film-maker, sugardaddy; art patron John de Menil; film-maker and Kinetic Theatre founder Carolee Schneemann; artist-writer Lil Picard; Andy Warhol; and superstar Ultra Violet. Admission is free.

age at the time of a broken
d which she initially assured
to have gotten very high on a
t of a seven-year plan also. My
uth fell open. She said what I
ew already however. The
ation of the world in seven
s. It was reassuring to be
roborated. But on February 22
ly says she felt too close to
th at the Grand Canyon in
66. We decide not to go by it.
er on she says oh shit we just
sed the Grand Canyon (to our
). Looking down at the Hooever
n or the Boulder whatever
y're calling it these times was
ugh for me. We're not any
ther away from home than they
. And we just broke the Genius
chine back in Arizona. You're a
ius if you score 700 and we left
ll fouled up at 843. Now we're
king about birthdates while she
ht be thinking about the
untains to the right looking like
s of pebbles, one on top of the
er my own thoughts she must
ncubating again or upset about
collaboration in the record
k I have her writing away
ously as I'm driving through a
storm and she says very old
od turns to stone in a million
rs or the hail is coming down in
special place and it looks like a
ser which is not interrupting
own excitement about the fact
t Jeannie's birthday, she said,
te it down hurry up, was June
so I'm now over the thoughts
ven the trees historically raving
ut the Magna Carta signed in
5 on June 15. June could be as
l a month as August. In August
all flip out. Or in. But on our
y out of Las Vegas Polly says we
uldn't look back, at the
ning city, and reminds me of
Sodom and Gomorrah story
ch George Segal now May 7, or

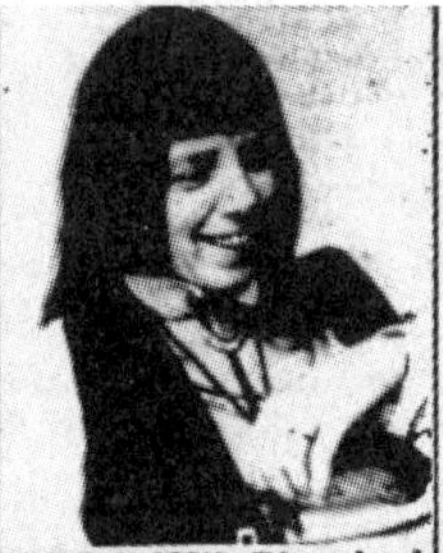

JILL JOHNSTON will be analyzed by John de Menil, Walter Gutman, Ultra Violet, Carolee Schneemann, Lil Picard, Dr. John Atchley, Andy Warhol, Gregory Battcock, and moderator David Bourdon in a panel discussion, "The Disintegration of a Critic," on Wednesday, May 21, at 8.30 p. m. at NYU's Loeb Student Center, 566 LaGuardia Place.

worldly interest for a friend: I wish there were more who would sacrifice their passions. The reason why two can do it is that each pretends for the other. This affair has long been a subject of gossip among magicians. Nobody even knows what virtuosos of imposture we are. We should marry our grown up dreams and stay behind the youngest still and sail our memories of home like boats across the Seine. These are the colors of my father's dreams says Judy Collins whose words Polly writes out to play also about the father who promised somebody according to Judy that we would live in France. The secret of the collaboration is out of the bag but Peter Hujar my photographer friend who tells me

point here, although I say to Teeny I think if she Alice didn't care for her it was because they don't have much in common; and if Gertrude got aggressive later on in life according to the pictures since I don't know them in person either it was because the two of them probably didn't have a dog to ward off any would-be intruders who wouldn't understand the collaboration. Pictures aside, in Spain I say to Jean Lanier the reason they made it at all according to Gene Swenson is how they got all stashed away in that house in Paris before anybody could do anything about it and I'm sure Leo was a good pal for awhile, like Theo was to Vincent under pressure of a blood relationship. That wasn't a solo trip either. It's hopeless. More than one of us arrived at a time. There's no end to these collaboratories. For instance I have a very special letter here, actually a photostat with handwriting on the back from a Pennsylvanian who lets me know he's thinking not only of me (he says he shares my appetites etc.) but of Sidney Lanier's namesake, I "missed a beautiful reference" he says, who was a "very interesting poet, flutist and composer of So. Carolina origins... his creative life straddled the Civil War, which, as a sensitive and cultured man, pained him deeply." The photostat is of "The Marshes of Glyan" by Sidney's father. I'm sending it to Sidney who was a priest once. I used to saturate the vestments of the priest in perfume myself. I was bad but the priest was old fashioned. That was 1947. I don't recall the day. I didn't have to polish the chapel brass for it anyhow. They didn't catch me. But I'm catching George Segal

Announcement from *The Village Voice*, May 15, 1969 for the panel discussion "The Disintegration of a Critic: An Analysis of Jill Johnston" at New York University, Loeb Student Center

JILL JOHNSTON will be analyzed by John de Menil, Walter Gutman, Ultra Violet, Carolee Schneemann, Lil Picard, Dr. John Atchley, Andy Warhol, Gregory Battcock, and moderator David Bourdon in a panel discussion, "The Disintegration of a Critic," on Wednesday, May 21, at 8.30 p.m. at NYU's Loeb Student Center, 566 LaGuardia Place.

PRESS RELEASE

Re Panel Discussion May 21st at Loeb Student Center of N.Y.U. "The Distintegration of a Critic -- An Analysis of Jill Johnston" with panel members David Bourdon (moderator), John de Menil, Walter Gutman, Ultra Violet, Carolee Schneemann, Bill Picard, Dr. John Atchley, Andy Warhol, Gregory Battcock.

My purpose in arranging this my third and last panel was to offer my name as a sort of sacrifice if you like for the idea(1) of a disintegration of criticism, which I view as an outmoded form of communication. Reportage may be necessary and interesting. I like it myself. Poetry and all forms of fiction, history, autobiog.y etc., I accept as forms of speech and writing not coercive as to the salesmanship of immediate artistic events, i.e., reviews in the newspapers and the magazines. A critic has come to be an unpaid publicity agent. The artist expects this of the critic and privately coerces him; the critic has accepted this role and uses the artist to build his own reputation: by the game of playing off one artist against another in the "historical sequence of trends." Anybody familiar with the history of art knows also how history is made by the winners of the moment: those with the power of money, press, fame etc., to urge an old artist on a new public, to resurrect a forgotten artist, to exhume an artist completely unknown to his own time even, to relegate to the grave a whole era popular for a time and so on. I am now interested solely in autobiographical history, from the cradles as well as from the history of an (our) archetypal past. As anything else I see both immediate and more remote history as imposed upon people from without and the people who take it as unwilling to accept the responsibility for deciding what their own history is, dependent always upon the judgment the authority of one who assumes it in the historical guise of the father of the Judaic-Christian patriarchal tradition. That this dependence will continue to exist I see as fated for the present yet equally fated to terminate in the near future, as a state of affairs family, educational and cultural and finally political. Having been a so-called critic I fall into the cultural category and the panel May 21st is meant to illustrate, as an art event of the "object lesson" variety, the demise of a particular critic who both literally and figuratively (or intellectually) disintegrated. In 1965 as I was hospitalized one aspect of my vision was in the form of a command to relinquish the role of judge, a role I never dreamed I would assume in 1950 in the first place, for in 1957 I was inspired solely to find a new language a new vocabulary for dance -- to make a new dance literature which I thought was historically and contemporaneously appalling. My first panel at N.Y.U. in 1968 was a conventional one with Robert Morris moderating. My second in the fall of '68 was a disintegration panel. I moderated and the panel members and myself relinquished our places to the audience. It was a "difficult" object lesson for everybody, us too, in the absurdity of authority. The panel May 21st is my final solution to a personal problem which I would hope to have some effect on all those caught in a similar trap if indeed they see it that way.

Press release by Jill Johnston for "The Disintegration of a Critic: An Analysis of Jill Johnston" at New York University, Loeb Student Center, May 21, 1969

PRESS RELEASE

Re: Panel Discussion May 21st at Loeb Student Center of N.Y.U. "The Disintegration of a Critic—An Analysis of Jill Johnston" with panel member David Bourdon (moderator), John de Menil, Walter Gutman, Ultra Violet, Carolee Schneemann, Lil Picard, Dr. John Atchley, Andy Warhol, Gregory Battcock.

My purpose in arranging this my third and last panel was to offer my name as a sort of sacrifice if you like for the idea(l) of a disintegration of criticism, which I view as an outmoded form of communication. Reportage may be necessary and interesting. I like it myself. Poetry and all forms of fiction, history, autobiog., etc., I accept as forms of speech and writing not coercive as to the salesmanship of immediate artistic events, i.e., reviews in the newspapers and the magazines. A critic has come to be an unpaid publicity agent. The artist expects this of the critic and privately coerces him; the critic has accepted this role and uses the artist to build his own reputation: by the game of playing off one artist against another in the "historical sequence of trends." Anybody familiar with the history of art knows also how history is made by the winners of the moment: those with the power of money, press, fame etc., to urge an old artist on a new public, to resurrect a forgotten artist, to exhume an artist completely unknown to his own time even, to relegate to the grave a whole era popular for a time and so on. I am now interested solely in autobiographical history, from the cradles as well as from the history of an (our) archetypal past. As anything else I see both immediate and more remote history as imposed upon people from without and the people who take it as unwilling to accept the responsibility for deciding what their own history is, dependent always upon judgment the authority of one who assumes it in the historical guise of the father of the Judaic-Christian patriarchal tradition. That this dependence will continue to exist I see as fate for the present yet equally fated to terminate in the near future, as a state of affairs family, educational and cultural and finally political. Having been a so-called critic I fall into the cultural category and even the panel May 21st is meant to illustrate, as an art event of the "object lesson" variety, the demise of a particular critic who both literally and figuratively (or intellectually) disintegrated. In 1965 as I was hospitalized one aspect of my vision was in the form of a command to relinquish the role of judge, a role I never dreamed I would assume in 1950 in the first place, for in 1957 I was inspired solely to find a new language, a new vocabulary for dance—to make a new dance literature which I thought was historically and contemporaneously appalling. My first panel at N.Y.U. in 1968 was a conventional one with Robert Morris moderating. My second in the fall of '68 was a disintegration panel. I moderated and the panel members and myself relinquished our places to the audience. It was a "difficult" object lesson for everybody, us too, in the absurdity of authority. The panel May 21st is my final solution to a personal problem which I would hope to have some effect on all those caught in a similar trap if indeed they see it that way.

Jill Johnston

JILL JOHNSTON will be analyzed by John de Menil, Walter Gutman, Ultra Violet, Carolee Schneemann, Lil Picard, Dr. John Atchley, Andy Warhol, Gregory Battcock, and moderator David Bourdon in a panel discussion, "The Disintegration of a Critic," on Wednesday, May 21, at 8:30 P.M. at NYU's Loeb Student Center, 566 La Guardia Place

Analysis by Lil Picard

CONFESSION WITH AN ACCENT

JJJJ/Jill James Joyce Johnston with a dash of Kerouac is a dry martini of a critic in motion, on a trip, a dancer with words, movement and changes. In the film "Changes" are passages which remind me of JJJJ's writing technique. She uses slow and fast motion. She uses abrupt changes. Gossiping associations and analogies in sign and shorthand abbreviations, staccato style. She is, so it seems to me, the only critic today who went on a word-trip, becoming miraculously creative. Instead of being an average, not-very-personal critic of modern dance, doing a typical traditional pedestrian Village Voice reviewing job, grinding out every week reviews on modern dance events and long, long paragraphs of writings, she started suddenly to become a dancer herself. She dances with words. She changed from Jill Johnston to JJJJ. I hope, Jill, you will understand that I mean the four-letter sign JJJJ as the greatest compliment I can give. James Joyce invented language as a changed world of thought. He also went on a trip into the inner spirit of the world of words and poetic abstractions.

Sounds, visual and thought-sounds, think-sounds: JJJJ's writing has the same quality.

ART

by LIL PICARD

She is
canny hi
wonderf
often as
sation w
I am
sophy-tal
New Yo
every u
—"Yes.

Sp

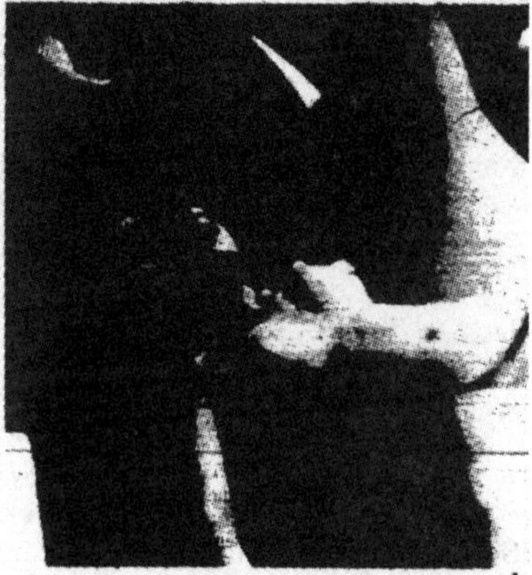

ph

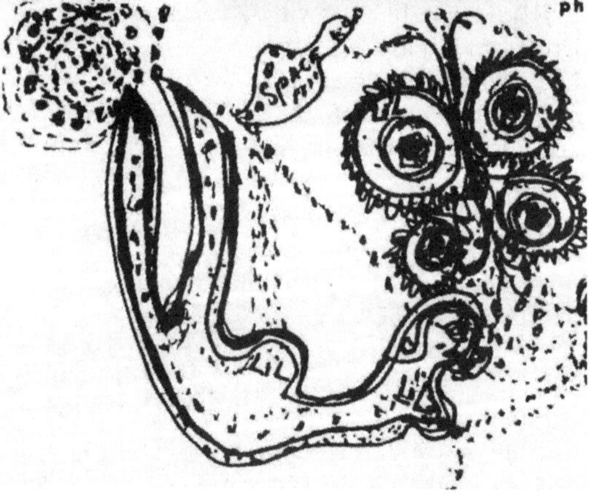

Lil Picard, "Confessions with an Accent," *East Village Other*, May 14, 1969

CONFESSION WITH AN ACCENT

Analysis by Lil Picard

JJJJ Jill James Joyce Johnston with a dash of Kerouac is a dry martini of a critic, in motion, on a trip, a dancer with words, movement and changes. In the film "Changes" are passages which remind me of JJJJ's writing technique. She uses slow and fast motion. She uses abrupt changes. Gossiping associations and analogies in sign and shorthand abbreviations, staccato style. She is, so it seems to me, the only critic today who went on a word-trip, becoming miraculously creative. Instead of being an average, not-very-personal critic of modern dance, doing a typical traditional pedestrian Village Voice reviewing job, grinding out every week reviews on modern dance events and long, long paragraphs of writings, she started suddenly to become a dancer herself. She dances with words. She changed from Jill Johnston to JJJJ. I hope, Jill, you will understand that I mean the four-letter sign JJJJ as the greatest compliment I can give. James Joyce invented language as a changed world of thought. He also went on a trip into the inner spirit of the world of words and poetic abstractions

Sounds, visual and thought-sounds, think-sounds: JJJJ's writing has the same quality.

She is very witty and has an uncanny humor. She is self-critical and wonderfully tough. Her writings are often as down to asphalt as a conversation with a New York taxi driver.

I am an addict to taxi drivers' philosophy-talks. They save my sanity in New York. One recently answered my every question with, "Yes, Fraulein"—"Yes, Fraulein," he said we went down West Broadway to 66 Grand Street. "Yes, Fraulein," and so I knew forever that I have an accent as an unchangeable external stigma. But I also knew that he liked my accent. I like JJJJ's personal accent of changes and motion. Yes, JJJJ, yes, American Fraulein.

What I want to say is: Jill didn't disintegrate as a critic. In fact, she got herself together and became a creative writer. I dig her. All the people she knows are dancers. Life is her group. She is a choreographer of the life dance. All her friends are action people. She dances with Polly, with John de Menil, with Jasper Johns, with Alice and Gertrude and Teeny Duchamp and George Segal. She pirouettes from personality to personality, from superstar to superbitch, without periods and commas in a stream of Virginia Woolf inner monologue subconsciousness all the way down the line of life. I am a frustrated dancer myself and clumsily I try to dance with words. Yes, Fraulein.

The only time when I get blessed with JJJJ's quality of word-dance-high is when I awake in the morning. Then I dream up a kind of dance orgy. Sentences become floating ideas mysteriously changing into associations. It is all like an extended dream trip, and I fly and feel free. I believe that what happened to Jill is that she freed herself of conventions and is now on a voyage in the dream dance of words.

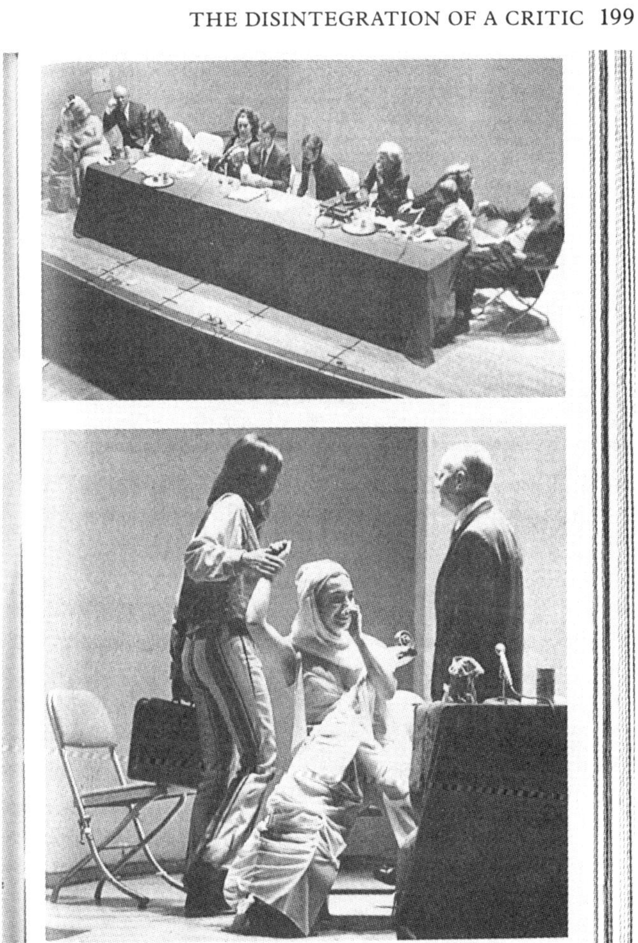

Page from Jill Johnston, *Paper Daughter. Autobiography in Search of a Father, Vol. 2* (New York: Alfred P. Knopf, 1985) showing the panel "The Disintegration of a Critic: An Analysis of Jill Johnston" at New York University, Loeb Student Center 1969: Charlotte Moorman, John de Menil, Jill Johnston, Ultra Violet, David Bourdon, Gregory Battcock, Andy Warhol, Bridget Polk, Lil Picard, Walter Gutman (top), and Jill Johnston's surprise appearance at the panel, with John de Menil and Charlotte Moorman (bottom), photos by Peter Moore

4

ANDY WARHOL

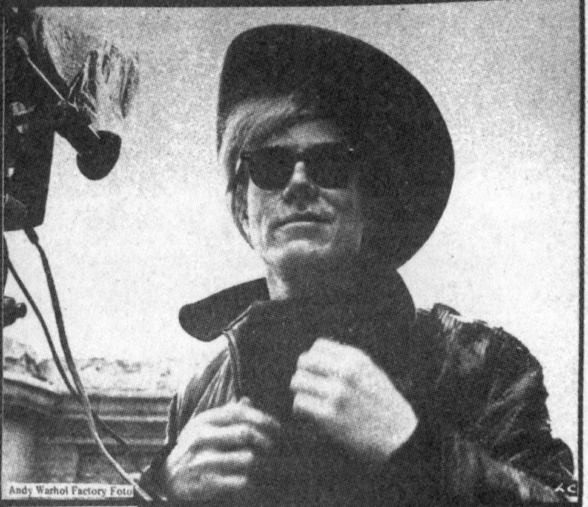

Andy Warhol Factory Foto

David: ... who has been reviewing dance for the Village Voice for ten years. Um, in the beginning Miss Johnston restricted herself to fairly routine dance reviews. Uh, after a short time, uh, she branched out to, uh, pursue more unconventional pursuits. Um, she was one of the first to recognize and write about the new forms of the medium, was one of the earliest and most sympathetic interpreters of Happenings in the theatre. Her critical writings played an integral part in the development and flowering of the Judson Dance Theatre in the early Sixties. Um, she never really specialized in so-called avant-garde or underground activities, never felt compelled to worry about what was going to be the going thing during the coming season, uh—in fact she was often unaware of what was ostensibly avant-garde. The reason that we do pay so much attention to her tonight and every night is that her past writings have proved to be so popular that we can't really ignore her. However, during recent years, her writing has become increasingly erratic. Her writing has become increasingly congested in style, extremely subjective in content, enormously [illegible] in its logic. It would appear that she has disintegrated personally and professionally on an enormous scale. Quite long ago, at least as far as I can recall, in fact, she ceased feeling any obligation to report on dance concerts. Um, no one can blame her for not wanting to waste her time reviewing the great number of conventional dance concerts that take place in the city. However, her column had, uh, so little to do with dance, even the rather far-out dance that she had promoted, that it became questionable just what she was doing writing under this Dance Column. The Village Voice was as mystified as anyone else. Um, those people in that marvelous little ivory tower over on Sheridan Square who are so aware of what's going on across the street from them, um, um, it took them a couple of years to catch on to the fact that Jill really wasn't reviewing dance at all. Around 1966 or 1967 they decided after months of contemplation to change the title of her column. They decided to call it Dance Journal, an ambiguous word that doesn't sound as if it has anything to do with criticism at all. Um, so we're here to discuss the personal and professional disintegration, um, um,—I'll begin with the personal first, which is probably more ... —maybe I should begin with professional, um, oh, um, well, ... Actually, she began writing this autobiography, um, sparing us very little of her personal life, though not giving us enough of the details to really make sense out of her column. Um, uh, her writing around the mid-Sixties began to include her sharply critical observations of people's behavior at parties and her perceptive comments on English cathedrals and lesbian works and any number of other subjects that appeal to her. She gave up any pretense of the third-person detachment that characterizes most personal writing, and began making intensive use of the first-person singular. As she began writing about her incredible life in weekly installments, she revealed to us a cliffhanger such as we had not seen since the Perils of Pauline. Um, her writing had always tended toward the subjective and in retrospect it was always autobiographical. She couldn't review a concert without telling us how she got there, what happened to her on the way, her trouble with the taxi driver, um—she never takes subways so she spared us that—um, she obviously saw her own travelling to and from the theatre as equally important as any of the choreography that she ostensibly went to review. I don't know how many of the people here are interested in Miss Johnston's personal biography. I've made several phone calls over the last few weeks to, uh, get certain facts on her, but I think I may skip that for now. Um, I would like to say that, um, uh,—about her writing—it really is quite, uh, real: her writing style is comparable to water from a faucet. Um, she turns it on a few hours before her column is due at the Voice, and, um, after a couple of hours she turns it off. Uh, she makes very few revisions. In her column she talks about notebooks. You might get the impression that she takes notes. Uh, I have seen her without a notebook, although she is usually writing down very elementary things like, uh, "Max's"—M-A-X-apostrophe-S. Um, I presume that many of the people here know all about her style, so I won't go into that, because I would like to mention that Esquire magazine last year did give her one of its dubious achievement awards, giving her the "Oh, Shut Up" Prize for the sentence which reads, "'Telling it like it is' means 'telling it like it was and how it is now that it isn't what it was to the Is Now People.'" Um, I do have—I spent the last months going through Jill Johnston's columns, and I have recalled a few sentences that she has written on criticism and I would like to read them. It's a timely subject which clarifies what follows later. Uh, the first one was written in her September 16 column in 1965 in which she wrote, "Criticism working out is like riding a bike up and down a country hill in a race against a phantom judge. I'll take a plot of level territory and stake out a claim to lie down on it, and criticize a constellation if that's what I happen to be looking at. I also stake out a claim to be an artist—a writer—if that's what I'm doing when I get to the typewriter and decide that I like something well enough to say what I think it's all about." Um, 1968 she said, "I like to think the critic is a corporate sensibility. Ideally the critic would be a transparent medium giving off vapors of ideas and opinions, constantly clasping to its body the stream of comments of cocktail parties. To mean exactly what you say that I mean, is to say that I mean exactly what you say that you mean, or any other variations on the phrase expressing the illusion of the single mentality. Collecting marbles, and , the critic is a scavenger of the junk gates of the mind, strung out from house to house in the telepathy of connected-connecting clotheslines, sorting out signals, selecting and conjecting, separating the pages back together is simply a compositional problem." You can see that she received ten dollars on that column. Um, in November 7, 1968, she wrote, "One of my preferences is to write about single things for each column. I like to work out a single thing into a mess of stuff about that single thing. I'm not crazy about trying to make a single thing out of a mess of stuff. Nor am I ..." Paul: Na na na na very good. David: One of her most illuminating pieces on criticism appeared this year—January 20, 1969. "I enjoy talking for the sake of my talking, until they say, 'Shut up,' and then I start thinking which can get you in trouble, too. What I am saying is not high-handed. When I criticize, I am never talking about anybody ever, in particular, actually—only myself ... except for my imagination or yours ... riding on a train ... the lost and found when I got there ..." Um, then, February 20, 1969 ... the end of criticism which she recalls in a serious article about criticism, she says, "I'm a critic myself ... plants and mountains ... they're all in my head ... a picture postcard ... not an original ... and I suppose it's true ... criticism ... illustrates ... talking about it ... talking about ourselves for a change ... whatever we're talking about is ourselves ... how everyone else is doing it ... I didn't mean to be called a critic in the first place ... three years ago I said that I was a cryptic ... what I started off was as a dance-lover just like that ... a long story ... the literature aspect of it ... dancer long before I was a true book nut ... although I read plenty of book stuff long before I was an athlete and a dancer ..." Those were just selections that I came across. There are a few questions that I would like to ask the panel on topics that I hope we will touch upon tonight, one of which is, uh—they're all so confusing, uh, uh, oh, one is "How Objective Can Criticism Be, Anyway?" ... um ... When Miss Johnston made the shift from third person to first person, uh, was she really in on something new ... um, and uh, things she doesn't want to—I forgot the vision ... where is the vision ... uh, in 1965, uh, she was under intensive care for, uh, for visions ... she had a— Paul: Very good ... David: ... she wrote that, "one aspect of my vision—" in quotes—"one aspect of my vision is in the form of a command to relinquish the role of judge." I hope that we will get on to that topic later and perhaps discuss her trip to Ann Arbor, via Houston, Santa Barbara ... Uh, I would also like to ask members of the panel whether they think Miss Johnston represents, uh, future criticism, and what sort of criticism we can look forward to, and uh,—I did want to make a few remarks about the merits and demerits of criticism, but I think I'll let that pass for now. I'm sure it will come out soon enough. So, I'll interview the panel beginning from my left. At my extreme left we have—this is a very distinguished panel, by the way ... not as distinguished as the audience—we have to distinguish ourselves—at our extreme left we have Walter Gutman ... Walter received a great deal of fame and notoriety a few years back which caused him to be profiled in the New Yorker magazine ... I am very happy to say have been reprinted by Grove Press ... —I received my copy two days ago—a marvellous book ... I recommend it to you all—look at it—Walter is—the real reason Walter was chosen for this panel is that he was a former art critic fifty or sixty years ago, and um, also a painter and a filmmaker whose career in so-called underground films goes back ... next to Walter is Lil Picard, an artist and writer and art critic of the East Village Other ... Lil has done many Happenings lately and is also destructionist art and street works ... she has written ... a fascinating show for this week's East Village Other which some of you may have seen ... sitting in the

Transcript of a recording of the panel "The Disintegration of a Critic: An Analysis of Jill Johnston" by Andy Warhol, published as part of his contribution for *Culture Hero Masterprint: Jill Johnston Exposed*, edited by Les Levine (New York: N.I.L.), 1970

ANDY WARHOL

David: *...who has been reviewing dance for* The Village Voice *for ten years. Um, in the beginning, Miss Johnston restricted herself to fairly routine reviews. Uh, after a short time, uh, she branched out to, uh, pursue more unconventional pursuits. Um, she was one of the first to recognize and write about the new forms of the medium, was one of the earliest and most sympathetic interpreters of Happenings in the theatre. Her critical writings played an integral part in the development and flowering of the Judson Dance Theatre in the early Sixties. Um, she never really specialize in so-called avant-garde or underground activities—never felt compelled to worry about what was going to be the going thing during the coming season, uh,—in fact she was often unaware of what was ostensibly avant-garde. The reason that we do pay so much attention to her tonight—and every night—is that her past writings have proved to be so prophetic that we can't really ignore her. However, during recent years her writing has become increasingly—erotic. Her writing has become increasingly congested in style, extremely subjective in content, enormously subtuitous in its logic. It would appear that she has disintegrated personally and professionally on an enormous scale. Quite long ago as long ago—as I can recall, in fact she ceased feeling any obligation to report on dance concerts. Um, no one can blame her for not wanting to waste her time reviewing the great number of conventional dance concerts that take place in the city. However, her column had, uh, had so little to do with dance—even the rather far, far-out dance that she had promoted—that it became questionable just what she was doing writing under this Dance Column.* The Village Voice *was as mystified as anyone else. Um, those people in that marvelous little ivory tower over on Sheridan Square who are so aware of what's going on across the street from them, um, um,—it took them a couple years to catch on to the fact that Jill really wasn't reviewing dance at all. Around 1966 or 1967 they decided after months of contemplation to change the title of her column. They decided to call it Dance Journal—an ambiguous word that doesn't sound as if it has anything to do with criticism at all. Um, so we're here to discuss* *the personal and professional disintegration, um, um,—I'll begin with the personal first, which is probably more ...—maybe I should begin with professional, um, oh, um, well, ... Actually, she began writing this autobiography, um, sparing us very little of her personal life, though not giving us enough of the details to really make sense out of her column. Um, uh, her writing around the mid-Sixties began to include her sharply critical observation of people's behavior at parties and her perceptive comments on English cathedrals and lesbian movies and any number of other subjects that appeal to her. She gave up any pretense of the third-person detachment that characterizes most personal writing, and began making intensive use of the first-person singular. As she began writing about her incredible life in weekly installments, she revealed to us a cliff-hanger such as we had not seen since the* Perils of Pauline. *Um, her writing had always tended toward the subjective and in retrospect it was always autobiographical. She couldn't review a concert without telling us how she got there, what happened to her on the way, her trouble with the taxi driver, um—she never takes subways so she spared us that—um, she obviously saw her own traveling to and from the theaters equally important as any of the choreography that she ostensibly went to review. I don't know how many of the people here are interested in Miss Johnston's personal biography. I've made several phone calls over the last few weeks to, uh, get certain facts on her, but I think I may skip that for now. Um, I would like to say that, um, uh,—about her writing—it really is quite, uh, real—her writing style is comparable to water from a faucet. Um, she turns it on a few hours before her column is due at the* Voice, *and, after a couple of hours she turns it off. Uh, she makes very few revisions. In her column she talks about notebooks. You might get the impression that she takes notes. Uh, I have seen her without a notebook, although she is usually writing down very elementary things like, "Max's"—M-A-X-apostrophe-S. Um, I presume that many of the people here know all about her style, so I won't go into that, because I would like to mention that* Esquire *magazine last year did give her one of its dubious achievement awards, giving her the "Oh, Shut Up" Prize for the sentence which reads, " 'Telling it like it is' means 'telling it like it was and how it is now that it isn't what it was to the Is Now People.' " Um, I do have—I spent the last months going through Jill Johnston's columns, and I have recalled a few sentences that she has written on criticism and I would like to read them. It's a timely subject which clarifies what follows later. Uh, the first one was written in her September 16 column in 1965 in which she wrote, "Criticism working out is like riding a bike up and down a country hill in a race against a phantom judge. I'll take a plot of level territory and stake out a claim to lie down on it, and criticize a constellation if that's what I happened to be looking at. I also stake out a claim to be an artist—a writer—if that's what I'm doing when I get to the typewriter and decide that I like something well enough to say what I think it's all about." Um, 1968 she said, "I like to think the critic is a corporate sensibility. Ideally the critic would be a transparent medium giving off vapors of ideas and opinions, constantly clasping to its body the streams of comments of cocktail parties. To mean exactly what you say that I mean, is to say that I mean exactly what you say that you mean, or any other variations on the phrase expressing the illusion of the single mentality. Collecting marbles, and , the critic is a scavenger of the junk gates of the mind, strung out from house to house in the telepathy of connected—connecting clotheslines, sorting our signals, selecting and conjecting, separating the pages back together is simply a compositional problem." You can see that she receives ten dollars on that column. Um, in November, 1968, she wrote, "One of my preferences is to write about single things for each column. I like to work out a single thing into a mess of stuff about that single thing. I'm not crazy about trying to make a single thing out of a mess of stuff. Nor am I ..."* Paul: *Na na na na very good.* David: *One of her most illuminating pieces on criticism appeared this year—January 20, 1969. "I enjoy talking for the sake of my talking, until they say, 'Shut up,' and then I start thinking which can get you in trouble, too. What I am saying is not high-handed. When I criticize, I am never talking about anybody over, in particular, actually—only myself ... except for my imagination or yours ... riding on a train ... the lost and found when I got there ..." Um, then, February 20, 1969 ... the end of criticism which she recalls in a serious article about criticism, she says, "I'm a critic myself ... plants and mountains ...they're all in my head ... a picture postcard ... not an original ... and I suppose it's true ... criticism ...*

*illustrates … talking about it … talking about ourselves for a change … whatever we're talking about is ourselves … how everyone else is doing it …I didn't mean to be called a critic in the first place … three years ago I said that I was a cryptic … what I started off was as a dance-lover just like that … a long story … the literature aspect of it … dancer long before I was a true book nut … although I read plenty of book stuff long before I was an athlete and a dancer …" Those were just selections that I came across. There are a few questions that I would like to ask the panel on topics that I hope we will touch upon tonight, one of which is, uh—they're all so confusing, uh, uh, oh, one is "How Objective Can Criticism Be, Anyway?" … um … When Miss Johnston made this shift from third person to first person, uh, was she really in on something new …um, and uh, things she doesn't want to—I forgot the vision … where is the vision … uh, in 1965, uh, she was under intensive care for, uh, for visions she had a—*Paul: *Very good …* David: *… she wrote that, "one aspect of my vision—" in quotes—"one aspect of my vision is in the form of a command to relinquish the role of judge." I hope that we will get on that topic later and perhaps discuss her trip to Ann Arbor, via Houston, Santa Barbara … Uh, I would also like to ask members of the panel whether they think Miss Johnston represents, uh, future criticism, and what sort of criticism we can look forward to, and uh,—I did want to make a few remarks about the merits and demerits of criticism, but I think I'll let that pass for now. I'm sure it will come out soon enough. So, I'll interview the panel beginning from my left. At my extreme left we have—this is a very distinguished panel, by the way … not as distinguished as the audience—we have to distinguish ourselves—at our extreme left we have Walter Gutman … Walter received a great deal of fame and notoriety a few years back which caused him to be profiled in the New Yorker magazine … I am very happy to say have been reprinted by Grove Press …—I received my copy two days ago—a marvellous book … I recommend it to you all—look at it—Walter is—the real reason Walter was chosen for this panel is that he was a former art critic fifty or sixty years ago, and um, also a painter and a filmmaker whose career in so-called underground films goes back … next to Walter is Lil Picard, an artist and writer and art critic of the* East

Village Other ... *Lil has done many Happenings lately and is into deconstructionist art and street works ... she has written ... a fascinating show for this week's* East Village Other *which some of you may have seen ... sitting to the right of Lil is Brigid Polk, a brilliant actor, best known for her very startling performance in the* Chelsea Girls, *um, she has another important part in the forthcoming* Imitation of Christ ... *she is also a very important artist whose media—medium is books ... she has about a hundred books which some of you may have read about ... she will soon appear on the cover of John Wilcock's* Other Scenes... *next to Brigid we have a young man who is impersonating the famous Senor Valdez ... um, and, um, who was very kind to come here tonight and we're very grateful, and next to him is Gregory Battcock. Gregory Battcock is famous for things so numerous I can't begin to mention them. Um, he did want me to say that he is an assistant professor of art history at Farleigh Dickinson University ... I'd like to mention the number of important books he's put out which I'd like to mention. And he's written articles for art magazines too numerous to mention. His most important job right now is that he is an art critic for the* New York Review of Sex, *doing a marvellous job there .... editor of Jill Johnston's forthcoming book* Selected Criticism From The Village Voice ... *Uh, to my right I have Miss Ultra Violet who is, uh, noted for a great many things like most of the members of the panel, uh, she is perhaps best known for her rather declining, persistent appearances on the Merv Griffith Show ... um, she is, of course, an actress who has appeared in many distinguished films, the most recent being John Chamberlain's* The Loves of Fernando Cortez *in which she made her screen debut, and uh, a .... of note ... and to the right of Ultra Violet we have another distinguished member of the panel, John de Menil of Houston and New York. Mr de Menil is chairman of an international company that specializes in oil fields for engineering purposes ... a very civic-minded man, a trustee of the Museum of Modern Art in New York, a trustee of the Museum of Primitive Arts, a trustee of the Museum of Fine Arts in Houston. And I would like to say parenthetically that he has one of the finest art collections in the United States that I have seen ... And to the right that strange Hindu apparition at the end is none other than Charlotte Moorman the heroin of much avant-gardey, the director of the annual avant-garde festival which has livened the city for five or six years ... famous performer and entrepreneur, uh ... a great deal of notoriety for her innovative performance ... modern musicians ... her interpretations of modern music have, uh, revolutionized cello-playing ... and that is our panel ... Now, would any member of the panel like to repudiate anything I've said? ...* A: *Who are you? ...* B: ... *and a former* Village Voice *writer ... Listen, I'd like to read Lil's column for today ...* D: *Brigid called me last night to read me Lil Picard's column in the* Last Village Other. *Uh, Brigid has this marvellous way of getting newspapers before they appear on the newsstands. She's always calling me up to read me columns weeks even months before the paper's out, and I was very impressed by Lil's column, and Brigid has such a nice since you're an actress you have such a nice reading voice, so you will read it, Brigid.* B: *This is an analysis by Lil Picard. "Confessions With An Accent." "JJJJ Jill James Joyce Johnston. With a dash of caraway is a dry martini of a critic. The emotions on a trip, a dancer with words. Movement and changes. In the film* Changes *are passages which remind me of JJJJ's writing technique. She uses slow and fast motion. She uses abrupt changes, gossipy associations and analyst sign and shorthand abbreviations. They call it style. She is, so it seems to me, the only critic today who went on a word trip being miraculously creative. Instead of being an average, not very-personal critic of modern dance, doing a typical, pedestrian, traditional* Village Voice *reviewing job, grinding out every week, reviewing on modern dance and long, long paragraphs of writings, she started suddenly to become a dancer herself. She dances with words. She changed from Jill Johnston to JJJJ. In my youth in Vienna, I was in love with the writings of Peter Altenberg and the short essays of Alfred Kubin. In Berlin in the Thirties it was the social critical writing of Chaomsky who wrote the most wise and witty political columns and small literary pieces ...* " D: *Give me the microphone. Move your chair up.* B: *The mike isn't on.* D: *No, it is on ... Gregory, I believe you have prepared a statement to deliver tonight. Would you like to deliver that statement at this time?* Gregory: *Well, uh, yeah, since you ask, yes, since I wrote it all afternoon, uh, to deliver tonight, and since I also happen to have it with me … A while ago Jill Johnston kept mentioning guacamole salad in her column … about the same time Clay Claiborne discussed a guacamole salad in one of this restaurant reviews … and about the same time the woman the* New York Times *refers to in their advertisements as Charlotte Curtis—rarely confused with Charlotte Moorman, although I don't know why not—talked about that guacamole salad that was served at a society luncheon. All three of these critics—Claiborne, Curtis and Johnston—have a lot in common. Each has recognized the inadequate limitations imposed upon thought by labels, but only Jill has managed to do something about it. Artificial categorization such as Art, Politics, Sex, have been eroded in her criticism—Freudian associations, free associations, personal and subjective responses to phenomena and cultural artifacts as well as artichokes have replaced them. All too frequently unnecessarily, the reader encountering the new criticism is left confused. For example, how many people still don't even know what guacamole salad is? Therefore, it is appropriate to begin with the definition of terminology … scientific method … and why shouldn't we, even though Marcuse tells us that the order and organization of class society … which has shaped the sensibility and the reason of man, have also shaped the freedom of imagination. Johnston is the only critic today with literary sensibility—another word for imagination … from the framework of her oppression … if the freedom of the imagination … by the sensibility as well as the directional faculty of man, then as we know, Jill is not sensible, she is not reasonable, and she certainly has disintegrated as a critic. However … none of her work is complete without a definition of guacamole salad … halve and peel one avocado and remove the pit … into small … and mash it … two tablespoons of lime juice … a quarter tablespoon of salt … and a dash of … pepper … I have no doubt … I can talk louder than you can hit, you know, so … genius performance at Judson Church … please stand up and take this, bow, or whatever … um …* D: *Gregory, would you like to finish that at a later time …* B: *… but I only did that because, you know, Jill hates cocks and she told me she was sick and tired of my cocks …* D: *Oh, you should say that in the microphone. Say that …* B: *… because Jill told me that she was soooo sick of my cock book, so I thought I'd give her my tit book now …* D: *… if nobody has any* *questions I would like to ask one. Ultra, as a fairly typical reader of* the Village Voice, *how do you think that Jill Johnston is so famous?* Ultra: *Well, uh, I wish that I knew Jill Johnston because you've talked so much about her and she seems to be really great … I met her twice and the first time I didn't know who she was, and she was terribly upset, and she didn't know who I was and I was not upset, and anyway I think I'm more famous than she is, but that's not the point … and I cannot like her and, uh, … go to bed with her … but I think that I really don't like the shape of her nose and her teeth—I think she should have her teeth done up sort of casual you know …* D: *Well, uh … Miss Johnston's dentist … um, Lil?* Lil: *Yes?* D: *If you won't read your column, do you think that what Jill is writing now, uh—her kind of writing—is what you would consider corrective to formalist criticism? Do you have anything to say about her—her writing? Not in terms of her style, which you dealt with, brilliantly … but could you say something about the content. Is she really, uh, leading us into something new …* Lil: *Oh, of course. Jill, uh, … changed … when she flipped out and became someone else, she wrote a very straight column on dance criticism and even art and art movies, and I think she was alright—I think she was … I never read art criticism because I think it's very boring … I can't read it … but when she changed she became very, uh, profound, because I think an artist ought to become profound in the moment he will not be understood by anybody …* D: *Well, I wonder if we can have a message from Charlotte on Jill's writing … Charlotte has been … by Miss Johnston on numerous occasions … over there … would you care to … Hello? Hello? Uh, could you say something about Jill? Maybe you could say something about her repertoire?* Charlotte: *I just want you to know that I personally agree with Walter Lippmann and Andy Warhol, and with you David … and who is Jill Johnston anyhow? …* D: *… Um, I'd uh, like to ask Walter something now because Walter was a working art critic many years ago, and is a very brilliant writer, and, uh, has a lot to say about women, and women who write, and some women who write, and, uh, whether he has any feelings about Jill's extreme subjectivity in her writing. Would you like to comment on her journalism … what seem to be her journal keeping, um … Do you feel that she puts too much of her psychology and her daily life into* *her column?* Walter: *... subjective ... But I still think that we should try to remember a little bit of Jill when she was a ... and I saw and recognized ... extraordinary powers of hallucination ... Jill explained the development of the dance from a long time ago until now ... I told her she should do more of this and publish it through ... this book on the dance which would have been a very fine book ... but she won't do this ... other feelings and other powers ... enable her to exploit her really really great mind ... what I'm trying to say is that she somehow expresses a large feeling of this time ... ten years ago ... many people haven't heard of her now ... what makes a writer isn't just their technical capability—of what she has a great deal ... that they do express more than ...* D: *Uh Walter? ... Walter? ... I would like to ask John a question now, and this is probably the question that concerned me most of all for a few years now, and that is, "Does Miss Johnston live her column?" Um, has it become a kind of substitute for her life? Uh, is it a kind of therapy that keeps her going from week to week—if she weren't able to practice her life in weekly installments, would she collapse completely, or has she some kind of fascinating vapor that passes through all of our lives to really ... crisis ... weekly chronicle ... ? That's a complicated question, but perhaps you can find something to say ... Um ... um ...* John: *I would not like you to take seriously what I am going to say because ... told me that ... institutions to be trusted ... and I think the question is ... and I'd like to challenge you for ... not having anything to hold on to ... I need three days to work from and since I didn't know that I was going to be asked this ... I'm not going to read a statement ... I can't read ... and I'll just give you three quotes ... one is special and it's from ... who said, "Anything that matters cannot be explained" ... another one is from one of the great writers of today and that's LeRoi Jones and LeRoi says, "Finally, it is deadly simple ... a point of view ... is of little value ... " And then with that extraordinary sense of poetry which he has, he adds, "Even air ... by the sun ... How can a man escape?" ... And sort of summing up those two I have another quote which is from Baudelaire. Baudelaire was an art critic from time to time ... and he wrote this: "I sincerely believe that the best criticism is that which is both amusing and poetic. Not a cold mathematical criticism which ... nor hate." And I think that with those three* *quotes we have Jill Johnston pretty well framed, because I think that she stems from the three of them. And, you know, a lot of things could be said about Jill Johnston, but there's more to her than all of them … I think that I can smell a rose … and when you said, David, but she has had "visions," I don't think she had "visions"—I think that she had "vision," which is totally different. Also you asked how objective can criticism be … I think that objective criticism is terrible—that the only criticism that is valid is subjective criticism and Jill Johnston started criticism in ballet, and, you know, ballet is so boring … it's soooo boring and it's so dead … How can she stay with that? She is alive. She cannot stay with a corpse … And then she started talking about what matters for her. And I think she is a person who is listening … I wish you could see all the books she's swiped from my bookshelves …* D: *About what you said about visions, I think that your criticism of my comment was very well made. I would like to retract that. I do believe that Jill Johnston has one big vision, and that each of her weekly columns are little fragments of that vision. John, you raised a very important point about, uh, criticism, and I think that, uh—you made a comment that criticism might be going in two directions—one of which is toward journalism, and the other of which would be in the style of Jill Johnston which is more of a literary sort of essay style, which is not founded in reportage so much. Jill never feels duty-bound to talk about what really happened to that week. She can write about what may have happened years ago … Is this new form of essay—I'm not sure that's even form—but will this be the future criticism? Gary?* G: *I don't know the question.* D: *We are speaking of Jill and her style of criticism—we haven't decided yet whether it's now or not, but, uh, it does seem that Jill has started something and, uh, perhaps other critics have picked up on her style of writing. Uh, certainly when I pick up* The Village Voice *these days I see that, uh, one of the regular columnists in it seems to be mimicking Jill's style—and not too successfully. I wonder if Lil Picard would have something to say about this.* Lil: *Oh, I was certainly influenced by Jill Johnston's turned on style … I'm very shy and I have an accent, so I don't dare … but the last couple of months I did there and I say certain things. I think that she turned me on to … I can get my personal feelings into the open. That's what she did. I think that to look at a work of art, you have to know how you react to it, what you feel yourself, and you have to question what art is today. You have to question what art is altogether, and Mr. de Menil mentioned that certain things that Jill Johnston wrote … I'd like to quote something that Jill wrote in* The Village Voice *October 17, 1968, and I'd like first to quote it as it is here because you mentioned … "there's no way to avoid murder, except by … murder …" … That's all.* D: *Well, um, another question that I would like to ask is, um, to any member of the panel—if any member of the panel would like to comment on it,—is "What makes Jill Johnston so often right?" I mean, why must we suffer this incredible prose—to hack our way through all these columns year after year, decided that she's kind of nutty, and then, years later, see that she really was right all along? Um, she's been very accurate about writing … one of the most important people of the Sixties, and, uh, her conclusions cannot be seen to be arrived at intellectually … they seem to be ruled by the fates. Uh, how does she—What does make her … Anyone?* John: *May I make a suggestion? We have a marvellous audience here of some three hundred people who obviously … Is there anybody in the audience who would like to answer that question?* D: *I have a question for the audience. I am very curious about how many people in this room have read through all of Jill Johnston's columns.*

the village VOICE, *May 29, 1969*

art

A SORT OF SACRIFICE

by John Perreault

Last Wednesday at about quarter after ten, sitting in the auditorium of Loeb Student Center at NYU, in the "press section," at a panel discussion called "The Disintegration of a Critic: An Analysis of Jill Johnston," I finally really understood Jill Johnston's writing for the first time.

I have always read Jill's column with great interest and lately more and more with considerable delight. Her writings on the Judson dancers turned me on to the new dance. Lately, as I am sure you have noticed, she doesn't write about dance or art at all. She just writes. Her writing has become increasingly elliptical and increasingly autobiographical. It is totally outrageous. Her columns are a skillful mixture of gossip, wisdom, name-dropping, trivia, mythomania, and shrewd observations. In some sense, she has become a visionary and this is both embarrassing and important.

As a person—and I have only recently gotten to know her—she is charming, impossible, delicate, aggressive. To say that she is totally nutty is beside the point. Who these days isn't? Myself and yourself included. There are, however, useful nuts and unuseful nuts. Jill Johnston's crazyness is useful. Somehow we must learn to tolerate our shamans. Middle class rationalism does not temper Jill's insights, pronouncements, denouncements, visions, nor on the other hand does it temper her temper or her panics. She suffers a great deal but she also enjoys a great deal She is a trouble-maker. She's totally impossible. You either love her or hate her. She's bigger than life.

For better or worse, a lot of us have been influenced by her writing lately—Gregory Battcock, Lil Picard, myself, and I'm sure there are many others. Oscar Wilde once wrote that the best and the worst criticism is always

Continued on next page

kindness) it is deliberate which | is recommended. The Hudson

John Perreault, "A Sort of Sacrifice," *The Village Voice*, May 29, 1969

A SORT OF SACRIFICE

By John Perreault

Last Wednesday at about quarter after ten, sitting in the auditorium of Loeb Student Center at NYU, in the "press section," at a panel discussion called "The Disintegration of a Critic: An Analysis of Jill Johnston," I finally really understood Jill Johnston's writing for the first time.

I have always read Jill's columns with great interest and lately more and more with considerable delight. Her writings on the Judson dancers turned me on to the new dance. Lately, as I am sure you have noticed, she doesn't write about dance or art at all. She just writes. Her writing has become increasingly elliptical and increasingly autobiographical. It is totally outrageous. Her columns are a skillful mixture of gossip, wisdom, name-dropping, trivia, mythomania, and shrewd observations. In some sense, she has become a visionary and this is both embarrassing and important.

As a person—and I have only recently gotten to know her—she is charming, impossible, delicate, aggressive. To say that she is totally nutty is besides the point. Who these days isn't? Myself and yourself included. There are, however, useful nuts and unuseful nuts. Jill Johnston's crazyness is useful: Somehow we must learn to tolerate our shamans. Middle class rationalism does not temper Jill's insights, pronouncements, denouncements, visions, nor on the other hand does it temper her temper or her panics. She suffers a great deal but she also enjoys a great deal. She is a trouble-maker. She's totally impossible. You either love her or hate her. She's bigger than life.

For better or worse, a lot of us have been influenced by her writing lately—Gregory Battcock, Lil Picard, myself, and I'm sure there are many others. Oscar Wilde once wrote that the best and the worst criticism is always autobiographical. If one reports one's reactions to a work of art—or to life—rather than describing or analysing, it is one's sensitivity and one's truthfulness that determines the worth of this confession. But back to the panel discussion. First of all the panelists did not arrive at the appointed time. Charlotte Moorman filled in the gap by sitting on the stage all wrapped up in pink cloth, as was her cello. By 9 o'clock I began to think that the bastards had really done it and that that the rascals were not going to arrive at all. I toyed around with the idea and felt comfortable with it and felt it appropriate given the announced topic, so at 9.05, when they began filing in, I was a little disappointed. It was an incestuous panel, just as this is, I suppose, an incestuous column. The panel: David Bourdon (Life magazine), was the moderator and was joined by Ultra Violet, Brigid Polk (of Cock-book fame), Walter Gutman, John de Menil, Gregory Battcock, Lil Picard, and Andy Warhol, who was introduced by Bourdon as a young man impersonating a rather well-known artist. Throughout Andy did not say a word, but occasionally used his Polaroid. To make a long story short, thanks to Bourdon's cool and sometimes cruel wit, everything was light-hearted and fairly entertaining. At one point Brigid took off her blouse. Gregory exposed his cock to Warhol's camera, forgetting that those in the balcony could see what was going on and began shouting "How big is it?"

This was the third in a series of panels organized by Jill and, yes, the topic "The Disintegration of a Critic" was her own idea. "My purpose," she write in her press release, "was to offer my name as a sort of sacrifice, if you like, for the idea of a disintegration of criticism, which I view as an out-moded form of communication."

At 10 o'clock the star of the evening appeared from the back of the auditorium. She was in her beads-vest-pants get-up, long hair flying, carrying her briefcase "Florence." She was smashed and all upset because her column had been cut. "It's all of one piece. It's a whole thing," she raved and then proposed to read the missing text, at first to the dismay of the audience dropped all objections. I politely hissed down Lil and Gregory for reading. After a false start—she was trying to locate the word "panic" which is where her column had ended—she began to read, and read, and read.

It was terrific. Her reading style, or perhaps I should say her performing style, is a mixture of Dylan Thomas, Ginsberg, and Edna St. Vincent Millay. The audience dropped all objections. I was moved. And so I finally really understood Jill's writing. Spoken aloud all the fragments fall into place. Jill is an orator and an evangelist. She is a poet. An old-fashioned poet, but a poet nevertheless. Jill Johnston not only dances, as Lil Picard says, she also sings.

THE LAST ESTATE

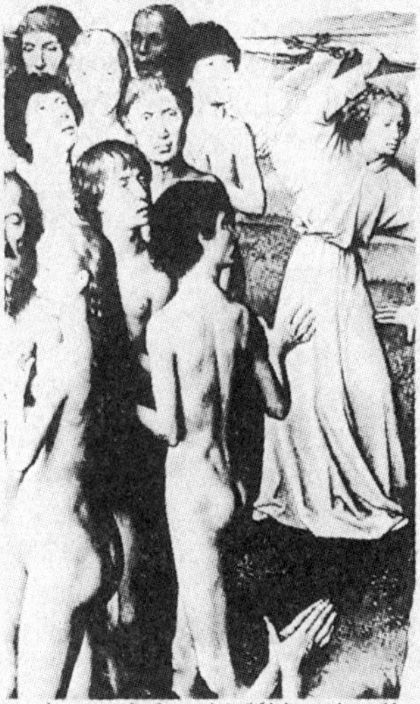

By Gregory Battcock

I was talking with Michael Benedikt the day after I got back from the French Antilles, and he said: Gregory, when you started writing for the New York Review of Sex you fucked yourself," and promptly submitted some of his really nice new poems to the paper.

Lately I've been complaining to the editor because my pieces were always stuck with horrendous photographs of open cunts and any matter of vulgarity. After my complaints, I started getting illustrated with line drawings from Beardsley and paintings by Crannach (I think) and my friend Bob the lawyer called me up and told me what happened at the Columbia pool when he went there for an afternoon dip. (I'll tell the point of this story ahead of time. It's that not only don't we know nothing about what is obscene and isn 't but we don't even know who to explain it all to.) Anyway, Bob marches into the pool stark naked–it's full of little children and one of the little boys has hair longer than the rest, Bob doesn't notice so you know the story, it turns out there's a girl snuck in somehow, but there's guys swimming naked so they got to get rid of her, they say, "little girl what you doin there, get out." She's all upset cries, can't imagine why she has to get out. Why should she I don't know, except I know that's obscene: making her go. Columbia doesn't deserve a new gym if that's what they do there. Gyms are what's wrong with education in America today-group sports are a substitute for learning in case you didn't know. The whole thing about learning is that the student is coming into contact with humanity but after five hours of gym who needs contact and the yearning for learning isn't the same

PATIENCE

"The disintegration of a Critic: an analysis of Jill Johnston," panel discussion at N.Y.U. on Wednesday night For ten weeks before the thing Jill is phoning every day so is David Bourdon, moderator. Nobody was sure who would show up though practically everybody did in the end. The panel, which consisted of Ultra Violet, John Menil, Lol Picard, Walter Gutman, Bridget Polk, Andy Warhol, Charlotte Moorman, me, is supposed to meet ahead of time

see a thing except for the people in the balcony who could. Bridget takes off her shirt, tits all over the place except the audience is again spared because this big ass table blocks the view. David goes on talking. The audience seems to really know what's going on, they don't want to hear nothing, hissing and yelling. I tried to read something clever I spent the whole afternoon in Riverside park working on, nobody wanted to hear it. O.K. What happened was important. I'd rather sit in the park and do nothing than almost anything else. I'm so busy sitting in the park that I have messengers deliver things, a messenger should have delivered my talk on Jill Johnston.

RIDICULOUS

Panels are ridiculous. Everybody knows that. So how

Gregory Battcock, "The Last Estate," *New York Review of Sex*, July 1969

THE LAST ESTATE

By Gregory Battcock

I was talking with Michael Benedikt the day after I got back from the French Antilles, and he said: "Gregory, when you started writing for the New York Review of Sex you fucked yourself," and promptly submitted some of his really nice new poems to the paper.

Lately I've been complaining to the editor because my pieces were always stuck with horrendous photographs of open cunts and any matter of vulgarity. After my complaints, I started getting illustrated with line drawings from Beardsley and paintings by Cranach (I think) and my friend Bob the lawyer called me up and told me what happened at the Columbia pool, when he went there for an afternoon dip. (I'll tell the point of this story ahead of time. It's that not only don't we know nothing about what is obscene and isn't but we don't even know who to explain it all to.) Anyway, Bob marches into the pool, stark naked—it's full of little children and one of the little boys has hair longer than the rest, Bob doesn't notice—so you know the story, it turns out there's a girl snuck in somehow, but there's guys swimming naked so they got to get rid of her, they say, "little girl what you doin there, get out." She's all upset, cries, can't imagine why she has to get out. Why should she I don't know, except I know that's obscene: making her go. Columbia doesn't deserve a new gym if that's what they do there. Gyms are what's wrong with education in America today—group sports are a substitute for learning in case you didn't know. The whole thing about learning is that the student is coming into contact with humanity but after five hours of gym who needs contact and the yearning for learning isn't the same.

PATIENCE

"The disintegration of a Critic: an analysis of Jill Johnston," panel discussion at N.Y.U. on Wednesday night.

For ten weeks before the thing Jill is phoning every day so is David Bourdon, moderator. Nobody was sure who would show up though practically everybody did in the end. The panel, which consisted of Ultra Violet, John Menil, Lil Picard, Walter Gutman, Bridget Polk, Andy Warhol, Charlotte Moorman, me, is supposed to meet ahead of time for a chat. We arrange to have a little wine and snacks at SHOEI on West 8th Street. Everybody arrives, and they start serving stuff at SHOEI except they're slow, but everything is exquisite. The sashimi, the tempura, the sake nice and warm, hot towels. The panel is at Loeb at 8:30. At 8:30 they're bringing us more Mersault at Shoei. David is a nervous wreck. Lil Picard sends out for some scotch. Andy is taking pictures with his new Polariod. So is Bridget but her's don't come out so good. More fantastic dishes come to the table. We can't tear ourselves away. It's nine o'clock already and still nobody is sure whether or not the panel will come off. Charlotte Moorman is missing. The hotel Paris they don't answer. Bridget orders more sake. Me too. And off we go.

Everything is extremely serious, but like the good lord said, if you don't mind, be so kind and unwind which we did. So we get to Loeb and the audience is all there, thousands of them waiting for only god knows what, we certainly didn't.

CHARLOTTE MOORMAN

Well who should be sitting up there. All by herself, and wrapped in a muslin shroud, but Charlotte Moorman and her cello, drinking beer out of a can wrapped in brown paper bags. The real question is when are the New York mothers really going to get with it, I don't know. With dignity, patience and a little drunkeness, everybody got up there and there weren't enough chairs. The audience is all there.

I see Ann Wilson who looks grouchy, sitting in the front row, Perrault is all there too, lots of people waiting and expecting the end all. Jesus. Any minute it could have turned into the Donald O'Conner Show, which is what we had to watch out for. They told me even Lee Steinberg showed up, not to mention all these people from the *Voice*, and a lot of people who looked like they were from Beanblossom, Indiana, maybe they came on a bus.

Well, David started things off fine, a lot of straight talk, everybody listened politely, somebody passed around a little bottle of bourbon, somebody else scotch, Charlotte had her beer, I had a little thing of sake still, The audience warmed up and started hissing, Andy says, "Gregory take out your cock so we can take a picture." so I did, and Andy and Bridget are snapping away, the audience can't see a thing except for the people in the balcony who could. Bridget takes off her shirt, tits all over the place except the audience is again spared because this big ass table blocks the view. David goes on talking. The audience seems to really know what's going on, they don't want to hear nothing, hissing and yelling, I tried to read something clever I spent the whole afternoon in Riverside park working on, nobody wanted to hear it. O.K. What happened was important. I'd rather sit in the park and do nothing than almost anything else. I'm so busy sitting in the park that I have messengers deliver things, a messenger should have delivered my talk on Jill Johnston.

RIDICULOUS

Panels are ridiculous. Everybody knows that. So how about a panel that is really ridiculous. Well, that's not easy. It has to be serious, have overtones of respectability. It has to be somewhat pompous, yet good taste dictates that, even if it is intended according to new, post-liberation values which don't exist yet include an outrageous mixture—unbelievable, unconventional, esoteric. It's quite possible that the most difficult subject for a panel of crickets to quiticize on is Jill Johnston because I think she knows all about "anti-criticism" which is like "anti-art in a way," it can be accomodated, within the traditional, prevailing institutions, procedures, marketplaces (I think—we don't know yet). That means it can't be analysed on a panel discussion at Loeb Student Center at N.Y.U.

The "anti-criticism" of freedom will meet with opposition and it will come, at least initially, from unexpected places.

The new hostilities, and I'm not going into this because if any reader has gotten this far, he surely has had his patience tried just about enough. Most everybody has by now, had their sensibilities progressively dulled by capitalist progress which is happily reducing the environment of freedom and the longing and need for such an environment. This is pure Marcuse without the footnote, and means that even such a simple thing as hostility can be viewed as a potential freedom that is reducible and has been denied.

Why live in a crowded city? Why live anyplace. The disintegration of the railroads coincided with the final collapse and disintegration of the cities in this country and it's amazing that rail transportation is still considered something else—not one or even part of the major areas of post-Vietnam-war concern. Rail transportation is an urban problem. The railroad made the American Cities, and like we now know, they were not only created by, but continued to depend on the railroad. Mercy, there's no point in crying city. That's not nearly the story. Sure, open spaces are nice, but they are not necessarily nice in the city.

Here is what Jill Johnston said (abridged) in the press release she prepared for this panel:

My purpose in arranging this my third and last panel was to offer my name as a sort of sacrifice if you like for the idea(l) of a disintegration of criticism, which I view for outmoded form of communication … A critic has come to be an unpaid publicity agent … the artist expects this of the critic and privately coerces him; the critic has accepted this role and uses the artist to build his own reputation: by the fame of playing off one artist against another … Anybody familiar with the history of art knows how history is made by the winners of the moment: those with the power of money …

ANTI CRITICISM

This then is what anti-criticism is. Today, the new artist must produce "anti-art"—that is, art works that are so opposed to the values and terminology of the mainstream of Western artistic tradition that they cannot be accommodated within the existing institutions; the prevailing values and criteria don't apply. In order to be awarded the "anti-art" label, these works must require different receptive faculties on the part of the observer; receptive faculties that for the most part haven't been developed yet. Obviously there is a problem. How can one even recognize anti-art when you see it. Well, usually you can't. As a matter of fact, it might well be the first criterion—at any rate a criterion for this time and place for art—that it not be recognizable, identifiable. that we not know it when we see it. That is, not know it's ART when we see it. Anti-art works must not only be difficult to accept as art, but they must be unacceptable as art. The anti-art notion doesn't stop with art, of course. All communicative forms must develop a negative, or "anti" expression. We must have "anti-journalism," which should not be recognized as journalism in any traditional definition of the term, an anti-fourth estate. And anti-criticism.

An "anti-art" must develop as it must accompany and more than that, it must create an over-all environment of true freedom. This is terribly important. It will meet with tremendous opposition—everybody thinks Jill Johnston is a quack, everybody respectable that is. Most of the antagonism to anti forms will, at least initially, come from unexpected areas, as I already mentioned. The new obstructionists against qualitative change in criticism will come from the same class who are now deploring violence and telling us we must all love one another ... the traditional liberal class is traditionally devoted to the protection of liberties within the capitalist system. This class is an unlikely adversary, and will be difficult to confront. At least the police and military wear uniforms and we can see them and we know precisely where they stand, guns, helicopters and all. The new obstructionists delaying the advent of revolution will come from a class that has, up until now, supported art, artistic freedom and has encouraged artistic license. However since "anti-art," (like "anti-journalism" and "anti-criticism") neither depends upon nor even cares about any of such traditional freedoms permitted within the capitalist class system, the liberal intellectual class that used to occupy itself with nothing at all to do—robbed of their only function with nothing to replace it. They are the kept intellectuals and they are housed today within the various liberal institutions that further and deliberately encourage intellectual elitism. One result from the inevitable reconstruction of the sensibility by the anti-worker will be an ending to the subtle class stratifications within the intellectual marketplaces. Grades, course requirements, degrees are already worthless. The university knows this, yet hangs on for dear life itself; however, let them hang on because they are dead already and it doesn't matter.

The anti-worker has to liberate himself from the prevailing terminology, classifications and categorizations. In criticism (quiticism) only Jill Johnston and Gene Swenson have, so far, been able to do it. In journalism SCREW, N.Y.R.S., GOTHIC BLIMP WORKS, OTHER SCENES have done it.

In art the "conceptual" artists have done it: so has Ann Wilson. In book publishing Walter Gutman has done it. "Anti-cinema" comes from Warhol; "anti-music" comes from John Cage. I used to tell the editor to stop putting shocking, perverted pictures next to my text. That was a stupid request and showed that I didn't know what was going on.

The editors would like to thank:

Andy Warhol Museum; Archives of American Art, Smithsonian Institution; Bakri Bakhit; Petra Bauer; Jon Chase; Stuart Comer; Timothy McDarrah; Fales Library, New York University; Louise Fishman; Gerard Forde; Gerda Henkel Stiftung; Roz Gerstein; Tatjana Günthner; Sofia Marie Hamnes; Liza Harrell-Edge (Evergreen State College); James Hoff; John F. Kennedy Institute for North American Studies, Freie Universität Berlin; Kunstbibliothek, Staatliche Museen zu Berlin; Mai Lahn-Johannessen; Les Levine; Justin Luke; Kristian Vistrup Madsen; Nick Mauss; Barbara Moore; New York Public Library, Performing Arts and Schwarzman Facilities; Andrea Niederbuchner; Ingrid Nyeboe; Ken Okiishi; Paula Cooper Gallery; Hilde Marie Pedersen; David Platzker (Specific Object); Yvonne Rainer; Sabine Reitmaier; Elizabeth Riordan (Special Collections & University Archives, University of Iowa); Maria Rusinovskaya; Jay Sanders; Saskia Scheffer (Lesbian Herstory Archive); Caroline Schneider; Felicity Scott; Steinar Sekkingstad; Jennifer Sichel; Jonas Skarmark; Skeivt arkiv, Universitetsbiblioteket i Bergen; Smith College Libraries Special Collections; Jamie Stevens; Bruce Tabb (University of Oregon Libraries); Einride Torvik; Maja Zahl; Stein-Inge Århus; and everybody at Bergen Kunsthall

Image Credits:

Page 9: Jill Johnston lecturing, undated, photo: Ralph Crane
Page 159: Jill Johnston on Gay Pride Day, 1971, photo: Fred W. McDarrah. Courtesy of Getty Images
Page 185: Jill Johnston at "Dialogue on Women's Liberation," Town Hall, New York, 1971, photo: Fred W. McDarrah. Courtesy of Getty Images
Page 192: Lil Picard Papers, Special Collections & University Archives, University of Iowa

All other images: the editors.